A French Flair

The artist, the gourmet, and the woman of fashion have always looked to France for inspiration. With the same zeal, knowledgable collectors have long regarded the art of French furnishings as the epitome of decorative chic. The craft of renowned French artisans has had far-reaching effects on civilized, cultured homes from one end of the globe to the other.

This invaluable guide by a noted authority lists all the great periods and the great names of French antiques, with information on all aspects of decoration from textiles to glassware.

For those who cannot afford the expensive originals but who desire to enrich their homes with the pristine beauty of French furnishings there are many clues to lesser-known, less costly antiques. The person of taste will also discover how a mood of graciousness can be achieved by authentic French touches throughout the home.

RUTH COSTANTINO is one of the foremost authorities on French furniture and decoration in America. A native New Yorker, she entered the art business in her teens. In 1923 she was called abroad to undertake the appraisal, cataloguing, and sale of a great European collection, worth more than one million dollars. In 1936 she founded The Connoisseur Inc., a Madison Avenue shop where she carries on a business in fine antiques; her clients include museums and art collectors both here and abroad. The widow of an Italian nobleman, Mrs. Costantino has two children. Her son is in the Foreign Service. Her daughter, HELEN COSTANTINO, the illustrator of this book, is an artist in her own right. She has had two "one man shows" at the Sagittarius Gallery in New York and is a graduate of Parsons School of Design.

SIGNET KEY and MENTOR Books of
Related Interest

How To Know
French
Antiques

Ruth T. Costantino

Illustrated by
Helen Costantino

A SIGNET KEY BOOK

PUBLISHED BY THE NEW AMERICAN LIBRARY

*I DEDICATE THIS BOOK TO THE MEMORY OF
MY LATE HUSBAND,
ARTURO ENRICO COSTANTINO.*

Contents

FOR FACILITATING MY RESEARCH I WISH TO EXPRESS MY INDEBTEDNESS AND THANKS TO MR. J. B. FRANCIS WATSON, MONSIEUR PIERRE VERLET, MONSIEUR R. A. WEIGERT, MONSIEUR JAMES BARRELET, MR. KARL KUP, MR. ARTHUR LANE, MR. W. B. HONEY, MONSIEUR Y. BRUN-HAMMER, CONNAISSANCE DES ARTS AND THE LATE COMTE FRANÇOIS DE SALVERTE.

AND FOR THEIR KIND PERMISSION TO REPRO-DUCE PHOTOGRAPHS OF THEIR PAINTINGS, TAP-ESTRIES, FURNITURE AND ART OBJECTS, I AM GRATEFUL TO THE FOLLOWING MUSEUMS AND COLLECTORS:

THE METROPOLITAN MUSEUM OF ART

THE FOGG ART MUSEUM OF HARVARD UNIVERSITY

THE FRICK GALLERY

THE SPENCER COLLECTION OF THE NEW YORK PUBLIC LIBRARY

MR. AND MRS. CHARLES ALLEN

MR. WALTER C. BAKER

MADAME CONSUELO V. BALSAN

MR. AND MR. GEORGE COUMANTAROS

MR. AND MRS. BENSON FORD

MR. RENÉ FRIBOURG

MR. AND MRS. EDWARD M. GILBERT

MR. AND MRS. ALEXANDER GOULANDRIS

MR. AND MRS. BASIL GOULANDRIS

MR. AND MRS. CONSTANTINE GOULANDRIS

MR. AND MRS. STAVROS S. NIARCHOS

MRS. MARIO PANZA

MRS. JOHN D. ROCKEFELLER, JR.

MISS EDITH STAMDEN

MRS. BRONSON TREVOR

MRS. ROBERT YOUNG

MR. R. THORNTON WILSON

AND SEVERAL OTHER COLLECTORS

PART ONE

CHAPTER ONE

Collecting French Furniture and Antiques

Through usage, the adjective "antique" has become a noun, and the word "antiquity" now implies an object of very remote times. The United States Custom House has fixed 1830 as the deadline, and any item (with the exception of rugs) produced prior to that date is considered an antique and may be entered into the United States without payment of duty. Rugs and carpets, however, are dutiable, unless they were made before 1700.

Many American so-called "antiques" are of later date, but since America is a relatively young country and there would be no question of importation, the definition of an antique can vary and the one-hundred-year-old piece might qualify.

With so long a history as that of France, things which were made after 1830 seem almost modern, but even there, as the fine things of the eighteenth century grow scarcer and more expensive by leaps and bounds, some young people furnishing their homes are now turning toward the nineteenth-century Louis Philippe period.

The art of France has always been so great and far-reaching in all its branches that it is most difficult to select the essential facts without wearying the lay reader with many dates and names. Without going into great detail, one cannot conscientiously cover the vast ground or do justice to France's enormous contribution to civilization and to culture. France has been in the vanguard since the Renaissance, and has been the cradle and arbiter of styles and tastes since that time.

I shall here try to present a general picture of France's furniture and decorations since her ascendancy, in order that the public interested in knowing "what it is all about" can form some idea of a subject which has fascinated and enthralled succeeding generations of people of good taste in all countries. To have a French salon or bedroom has been the ambition of fashionable people from one end of the globe to the other. Not only in Europe, but even as far as Egypt, Turkey, and the South American countries, the glamour of French furniture of the eighteenth century is recognized as the height of elegance.

Collecting antiques is a most delightful and rewarding hobby and one which can be enjoyed at any age. It provides a cultural interest long after other entertainments have begun to pall. A true collector is never bored. When he is not actively searching he can be reading and studying, and he will never cease to learn.

Some may regard collecting as a rich man's pastime, but many people of limited means are able to find lovely things within their reach if they do not concentrate on the periods most in vogue. Furthermore, many collectors have had the exhilarating experience of finding that what were regarded as their greatest extravagances in the past have proved to be their soundest investments. What could be more delightful than to indulge oneself in the purchase of beautiful things and to find that one has augmented one's worldly wealth in the process? To surround oneself with beauty is a wise and salutary thing to do and in the present economic state of world finance it can be done with a clear conscience, with the knowledge that one is serving the interests of one's heirs rather than depriving them of their inheritance.

In America we had a group of great collectors in the late nineteenth and early twentieth centuries to whom we owe a great debt of gratitude for having left their splendid collections to our museums, where we can study and enjoy examples of France's decorative arts at their best.

In this age of simple living, with no servants and with

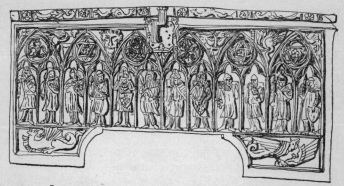

Fourteenth century carved woodchest. Musée de Cluny

ceilings in new houses constantly losing altitude in exact ratio to the increasing height of the already tall Americans, provincial furniture is often more appropriate than the elaborate type intended for high-ceilinged palaces with liveried servants.

Many people in America are under the erroneous impression that "French provincial" means furniture of the Louis XV period. Actually, it describes any furniture made

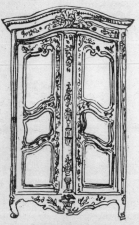

Provincial Louis XV *armoire* (c u p b o a r d)

Louis XV provincial *garde manger* (food cupboard)

in the provinces, in any period. Provincial furniture is readily distinguishable from the sophisticated Paris type by its simplicity of design and material. It was made of solid wood such as walnut, oak, fruitwood and, under Louis XVI, of mahogany. Except when produced by such outstanding cabinetmakers as Hache of Grenoble, Demoulin and his sons of Dijon, veneers and marquetry were not usually employed for provincial furniture. Most Paris chairs were made of beechwood during the Louis XV period, but Nogaret of Lyon, who was one of the best *menuisiers* outside of the capital, often used walnut. Provincial furniture is often very charming in line and finish, especially when based on Paris models. But when made by a carpenter instead of a cabinetmaker it is relatively coarse and clumsy. Because of its great popularity, provincial Louis XV furniture has been reproduced in great quantity both here and abroad. There are also many reproductions of the more elegant Paris furniture on the market, some of which, of excellent workmanship but of questionable taste, were made in France in the nineteenth century.

Spurious antiques flood the market. If one could explain in a few lines or even within the covers of one book how to distinguish between a genuine piece and a copy, there would be no need for an expert to devote most of his life to learning and observing. However, there are a few hints which might be helpful in avoiding some of the pitfalls. A copy almost always varies from the original in some way, as each generation produces things according to its own

Modern copy of
Louis XV caned chair

Victorian copy
of Louis XV
side chair

conception. A Louis XV chair or table made in the Victorian era looks Victorian to a trained eye, while a reproduction made today shows the modern influence. In the nineteenth century, reproductions were made very painstakingly and without regard for the number of hours expended. True, plaster ornamentation frequently replaced that which would have been carved in the eighteenth century, but generally the well made pieces came much closer to the originals than do modern copies, made by machine with a minimum of expense in labor and materials.

It has always amazed me that, with all the fine furniture to be seen in museums and even available in the open market, so many pieces are copied from very poorly designed models. Aside from the all-important goal of cutting costs, this is due partly to the present-day liking for things that look quaint, and their modification to suit the demands of the public. Louis XV and Louis XVI commodes now appear as double commodes with the "hers" and "his" motif much in evidence. Bedside tables are enlarged and distorted to accommodate radios, telephones and all the paraphernalia which make for present-day comfort. Meanwhile the original style is completely lost in the process.

The presence of nails and screws in antique French furniture should immediately arouse suspicion, as none were used in the construction of the period. Furniture at that time was doweled and edges dovetailed. Nails or screws are a sign that the piece is either spurious or that it has been inexpertly repaired. Unfortunately, many beautiful things have been mutilated by rough and inexperienced repairers through the ages.

Wormholes, which many people look for and expect to find, are not an indispensable sign of age. Some very fine furniture has come down through the centuries without any sign of the ravages of worms. Wormholes, unless manmade, are always pinheads of varying sizes, rather than uniform as when made by a shotgun. A more efficient tool in producing an uneven effect is a dentist's drill which is now used by imitators. Furthermore, worms never expose their channel on the outside of a piece of wood, therefore if channels are found on the exterior it means one of two things: either the wood was so completely eaten away under the surface that the outside collapsed and the piece had to be planed down, or else the piece was made of old wood from some other source. You cannot recut worm-eaten wood without running into such channels. Frequently such havoc is wrought by worms under the surface that what appears to be a sound piece is like cork or powdered wood in its interior.

Many people erroneously believe that a piece of furniture made of "old material" has more quality than it would otherwise have and are proud of it for that reason. Perhaps the finish is more mellow than that of a piece fresh from the factory, but actually, this form of forgery does not enhance value above that of a frank reproduction; although it might very well fool the inexperienced eye.

There is no royal road to recognition of an antique. The best possible method is that of looking and observing carefully on every possible occasion and studying the shapes, lines and general aspect of pieces of unquestioned authenticity. Experts examine pieces very carefully, from every angle and upside down, as well as the insides, backs, and carcases of cupboards, cabinets, and commodes. A sense of touch is helpful in judging antiques for long use gives a smoothness which cannot be produced artificially. Even the color of wood on the underside of a chair tells a story. Some gilded chairs were painted a yellowish color before the gesso and gold leaf were applied, a treatment which masks the original wood color and makes it necessary to look for other signs. In America, upholsterers have a bad habit of finishing the underside of a chair with a black cotton material to cover the webbing. This is a great obstacle in examining a chair.

Even if one is sufficiently expert to recognize the difference between the real and the spurious, which takes years of experience; one must be careful in purchasing sets or even pairs of chairs to make certain that all of them are genuine. Often there are only one or two antique chairs, which have been copied to form a set. This is especially true of dining room chairs, which are extremely hard to find in the required number. There is nothing wrong with using good reproductions where the real thing is unobtainable: the point is to know what one is getting and to pay accordingly.

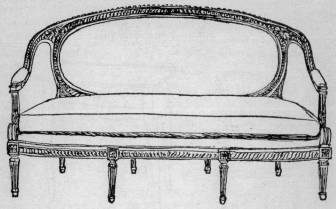

Canapé and *fauteuil* from a Louis XVI set by Louis Delanois and Sulpice Brizard (Metropolitan Museum of Art)

However, it is not at all unusual when finding a set of genuine chairs of the period to discover a number of different signatures, or no signature at all on some pieces and two or three different ones on other chairs or on the matching *canapé*. In the eighteenth century when work was done so meticulously by hand it took a great deal of time for one man to finish a set. A cabinetmaker employed other men to help him and the work was divided. It also happened that a householder might want more chairs after the first were already in his possession. Then he ordered more, which were not always executed by the same hand. This accounts for the slight variations in details to be found in sets, but there is no drawback whatsoever in any of these differences nor is there any lessening of value as a result.

Louis XVI *bergère*

Louis XV provincial table
with legs cut down

Bergères which were originally made in pairs and are of greater value as such, have frequently been separated when a parent, foolishly determined to show no partiality toward either of two children left one to each. Thus, they were separated forever, reducing their value and doing a great disservice to posterity. In order to restore them to a pair, modern cabinetmakers have made copies, more or less accurate, which can easily fool the unwary.

Very few commodes were made in pairs in France during the eighteenth century, so their appearance in the market should immediately arouse suspicion and warrant most careful examination. One, if not both, is very likely to be a copy. Until as recently as ten years ago, when some low quality but genuine commodes could still be purchased very cheaply, clever cabinetmakers bought them for the old material they contained. If the shapes were good they were either redecorated with new marquetry or covered with old Chinese lacquer panels, most skillfully applied to the original carcases. A real master of this fraudulent practice died only about two years ago, leaving a great number of such pieces behind him.

There are natural areas of wear on every piece. Edges of tables grow smooth and slightly rounded from constant dusting and use over the years; the place where the hand rests on an arm chair shows worn carving or old paint. The great humidity in which many pieces have stood for generations has rotted away the feet of cupboards and the hoofs of chairs. These are frequently repaired and replaced, but an extremely meticulous amateur or expert shuns such pieces unless they happen to be of such unsurpassed beauty and excellence that he prefers to overlook the defect rather than deprive himself of an outstanding example. One can forgive a defect in a piece of furniture one loves, as one does in a human being, provided the other qualities and charm outweigh it. And one must never insist on the sort of perfection that is to be found only in furniture straight from the factory.

As I mentioned before, there have always been inexpert repairers who have done more harm than good. Chairs originally made for caning have often been upholstered and the upholstery tacks driven right into the wood frame. With the present craze for low tables, legs have been cut down, aprons eliminated, and many painful surgical operations undertaken that have always resulted in the death of the victims. It would be well to assume that each piece was thoughtfully designed and its proportions carefully studied at the time it was lovingly made by hand.

If bursting with creative fancies, I strongly recommend that the budding would-be artist start from scratch and order a new piece in accordance with his views of how it should be made, rather than mutilate the relatively few existing authentic pieces. This includes the horrors in the form of lamps which one sees wherever one goes, and all types of adaptations to whatever we consider necessary to our comfort.

Period faïence and porcelains are very difficult to know because the old patterns have been copied over and over again. It is difficult for the amateur to distinguish an original piece made at the time the type first appeared from an exact copy of later date. Were it possible to see the genuine piece and the copy side by side, the student would be amazed at the lifelessness and dullness of the copy as compared to the original. But since it is almost impossible to find the two to examine at the same time, one must look for spontaneity and life in the painting of a plate, for example, and the right texture and color of the "paste" of the porcelain or faïence itself. The outstanding characteristic of authentic pieces is their brilliance and life.

If carefully observed, one notes that antique silver is slightly different in color from modern, and the silver of different countries varies according to the alloy used in its composition. Silver generally bears a hallmark, but not all hallmarks are genuine. A method of transferring hallmarks from an unimportant piece such as a fork or spoon to an important vessel, has been discovered and is unfortunately practiced a good deal. More, I am inclined to think, on English silver than on French, as there are more odd, expendable English pieces to be found with which to perpetrate the fraud.

Textiles have been and are constantly being copied from the old. Some are magnificent and fabulously expensive, but nonetheless they look as modern as they are. Before the machine age, vegetable dyes were prepared by hand and the silks handwoven, which resulted in a certain life and brilliance which we do not seem able to duplicate today. However in Lyon, France some splendid copies of the antique are being made by hand which may confound future generations. But just as an expert can recognize a nineteenth-century copy of an eighteenth-century silk or velvet, so I feel certain that the twentieth-century fabrics will bear their own telltale earmarks, no matter how conscientiously they are copied.

Spurious paintings are frequently painted on old canvases and for centuries worthless paintings have served this purpose. The imitations were painted in the style of some great and popular master, and were the more convincing because of the genuine period canvas. The world is full of false Bouchers, Watteaus, etc., and there was a painter in Rome who turned out charming Francesco Guardis as if he were a factory. He had studied and developed Guardi's style and idiom until it became his own and he was able to give his work the freedom that is rarely found in a copy.

Even drawings are faked on old paper, and one of the most popular ways of making a duplicate of a good charcoal or sanguine drawing is the system of transfer. When the original charcoal or crayon is heavy enough to come off on a second sheet of paper tightly pressed against it, an exact duplicate in reverse is the result. But it is not considered an original, and its value is nominal. This method has been used for hundreds of years, since faking has been done through the ages.

Bronzes are probably one of the most difficult categories to judge. Of course the threads of the screws must be made by hand, and the whole design and workmanship must have the characteristics of the period in which they were made. The gilding, too, tells a story, but since even some genuine pieces have either had their gilding spoiled or been regilded, one cannot always use that as a criterion of authenticity.

The question of taste has always been controversial. There is a Latin saying, and one in French as well, that tastes cannot be discussed or disputed. Nevertheless, it is a fascinating subject on which people differ greatly, and much has been written and said in an attempt to define it. It seems that, above all, a certain innate refinement and knowledge are indispensable requisites, before even attempting to consider the problem. Instinct alone is not enough. "I don't know anything about it; I only know what I like," is a remark heard very frequently. This is often said defiantly, as though the speaker wished to disassociate himself from so unsavory and pedantic an accomplishment as real knowledge.

The tastes of many people are based largely upon association, and their subconscious memories influence their likes and dislikes. If as children they were bored or unhappy in certain surroundings, they react against similar ones later in life. Just as an odor awakens memories, so the atmosphere in a house or a room reminds one of pleasant or unpleasant experiences.

It seems very unflattering to parents that so many people thoroughly dislike the type of decoration in which they were raised. When furnishing a house of their own, they want to get as far away from their parents' taste as possible. On the other hand, they frequently boast of their grandmother's possessions, which they hold in far greater esteem than the objects themselves merit. Perhaps they are pleased with the thought that they had a grandmother of substance, sufficiently well-placed to have left some mementos.

Although beautiful pieces remain beautiful under all

circumstances, there are modes and fashions in antiques as in everything else. Some of the changes are due to the difference in construction, for it is impossible to house large sumptuous pieces in the new low rooms now being built. When the fine pieces of one popular period are impossible to find, or are priced so high that very few people can afford them, the decorator is obliged to turn his imagination into other channels and launch a style that he can find on the market and that his client can afford.

The expression *nouveau riche* is uncomplimentary, and opprobrium is attached to the term *parvenu*. This is quite unfair. What would have become of art had there been no new rich to encourage and foster it and to support the artists? The man who has earned his money himself is not afraid to spend it. He knows how to go about getting more.

In the process of collecting he is learning and, since he is probably clever, even if he may never before have concerned himself with the subject, he learns fast and is a sincere acolyte at the altar of art. Its acquisition not only gives him a social position which he could not otherwise acquire in less than a generation, but he also begins to appreciate and love fine things for their own sake. Eventually, even without previous experience in the field, he can become a very astute and keen connoisseur.

The great nobles of yesteryear were *nouveaux riches* in their times, only fortunately for their descendants, it was long enough ago to have been forgotten. Nobody quarrels with the acceptance of their attitude of superiority, although frequently their sole claim to distinction is that their ancestors were robber barons or successful soldiers in the distant past. When, a few hundred years ago, a man was invested with a title and lands, he invariably set to work to build the most splendid castle, château, or estate within his imagination and his means. How does he differ from the new rich of today? More often than not the old aristocratic families with their effete culture have lost the vitality of their ancestors. Some have been living for years on the sale of their accumulated wealth and treasures. It seems to me that the difference between the rich and the new rich lies in the manner in which they spend their money. With longer experience the old rich acquire better taste and generally spend more gracefully. But this is not always true, especially when a person with newly acquired wealth makes a serious study of art in all its forms and acquires a certain culture in a very short time.

Many people who acquire money suddenly and want to surround themselves with luxury engage a decorator to produce a lush and expensive setting. Here in America they usually begin by spending a fortune on bars, fancy kitchens, gold-plated bathroom fixtures, thick wall-to-wall carpets and window draperies that not only spill over on the floor to produce a lavish effect but also cut off all the light so highly prized, advertised and paid for. Good exposures count for naught, since fresh air, free of the fumes of the streets, which can only be enjoyed on the upper floors in most big cities, is entirely shut off and air-conditioned. With artificial light used almost exclusively, one might be living in a cave! Afraid of being vulgar, these people shun color. They love it, but are afraid to demand it of their decorators for fear it will spoil the quiet, dignified atmosphere they are seeking. So beige, white and pastel tones are what they get, with an occasional "accent" (as it is called in decorator parlance) of color. They want to be refined at all costs. After spending so much money on carpets, draperies, and gadgets, there is not enough left to buy good furniture or paintings.

It takes another ten or fifteen years of prosperity for these people to learn the error of their ways, were they to sell out their entire possessions they would receive practically no money for them. If they then threw everything out and started over again, they may have learned a good deal and acquired a new approach to works of art. The second time around they might become real collectors.

One often hears people speak of a collector with pitying superiority because he has paid a high price for some picture or piece of furniture. Actually, instead of demonstrating his lack of acumen, it proves the reverse. A bargain in the antique field is generally an object of little or no real interest. It is possible to buy an object of ordinary or medium quality at less than its usual market value, but what interest can a collector of very fine pieces have in that sort of deal? Today's expensive pieces are probably tomorrow's best purchases, as the values of fine things rise in proportion to their rarity. A wise collector, such as J. P. Morgan, is not niggardly about price and can face with equanimity the fact that the seller is making a profit. Indeed, unless he is willing to do so, the dealer will not even show him his best pieces.

If young people furnishing on a budget say that a less nice piece will do or will answer their purpose, it is quite natural. But a collector who wants the best should never settle for less. If a man has the means to collect, what difference does it make to him if he pays more than he planned, if he gets the piece he really wants? If, through his keen business sense, he misses a piece which would give him infinite pleasure, he may never again find one as fine. The money saved will probably play no role at all in his position and he has deprived himself needlessly of an enduring pleasure.

The case of a society woman's deal with Cartier's many years ago has been the subject of much talk. For a pearl necklace she longed to possess she traded a building on Fifth Avenue in New York which she did not need nor wish to use. The fact that the building's value rose, while that of the pearls decreased, has shocked people. But why must a woman of great means make a profitable deal when satisfying a desire for some luxury she craves? And why are jewels and antiques purchased as assets or investments, when no other luxuries in the world are expected to increase in value?

This lady's attitude was right. She wanted the pearls; she did not want the house. So she made an exchange which gave her what she wanted at the time she wanted it. Since man is not immortal, how can one doubt his wisdom in satisfying an aesthetic craving during his short sojourn on earth?

People are often very definite about what a piece should cost. How can they decide that? A good piece is not worth just a little more than a bad, nor is a fine piece worth just a certain amount more than a good one. Each is in a separate category and must be considered from an entirely different aspect. It is not simply a case (to paraphrase Gertrude Stein) of "A table is a table is a table."

An interesting phenomenon is that of a man who has amassed a fortune through his own efforts and who is presumably a shrewd judge of human character, but suddenly falls prey to flattery and the sales talk of smooth, obviously unreliable dealers, whose equivocal characters are apparent to all outsiders. What causes this metamorphosis in a brilliant businessman? Is it that he loves the flattery and is willing to pay for the fairy tales which he wishes to believe? I wonder how rich a man must be before he reaches this point and loses his judgment.

A humble approach to a work of art is of great value in developing a flair for judging, and real knowledge. Too often, after a relatively short experience in collecting, people feel that, armed with a smattering of information gleaned here and there, they have mastered the situation and understand what they see. The sincere student should let the piece in question speak for itself, instead of projecting his own personality into his manner of observing it.

The fact is that one must develop a sixth sense in judging antiques and, curiously enough, with patience and persistence one does. At first glance a piece is either convincing or the reverse, and the best advice I can give anyone is: If in doubt, leave it alone. An instinct or hunch is a gift which must not be ignored. But it frequently is, because it is human nature to do so when one wants to have discovered a treasure. This is certainly one way to learn, but an expensive way.

PART TWO

CHAPTER TWO

The Renaissance and Louis XIV

French furniture, to the average layman, means that of the eighteenth century, and he conjures up a picture of the furnishings of that period. But the civilization of a great country like France can be considered to have begun with the Merovingian kings in the fifth century. There are very few pieces of furniture in existence that antedate the Gothic period, and as these are well documented in museums, there is no need to dwell on them here.

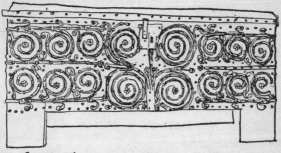

Seventeenth century chest (Musée Carnavolet, Paris)

Life in the fourteenth and fifteenth centuries was austere and often grim. It was a time of high religious devotion, and choir stalls and church furniture of that time show with what great fervor the artists and artisans worked on

23

their imaginative and magnificently wrought creations. The most fundamental and most prevalent piece of furniture of the early Gothic period was the carved wooden chest

Late fourteenth century choir stall with linenfold carving

which served as a seat, a storage place for clothing and linen, and as a trunk if the owner moved. The design of these chests, and of the relatively few cupboards, was inspired by the architecture of the day and these pieces were

Fifteenth century chest (Musée de Cluny, Paris)

very like the buildings, on a reduced scale. Until the fifteenth century the covers of chests were flat, but when stools and chairs became numerous, chests were no longer required as seats and from then on their covers became domed and rounded. Ironwork reached a state of high perfection and was at times handled with the delicacy and refinement more often reserved for precious metals. Wrought iron locks, similar to those on doors, were often mounted on red velvet to protect the wood of the chests

Early sixteenth century chest,
transition from Gothic to Renaissance

under them. The genuine pieces of Gothic furniture still in existence are largely in museums and old private collections.

Oddly enough, amidst the somber decorations of the Gothic period, there appeared the most sumptuous, colorful and magnificent textiles, which lifted the whole scene from one of gloom to great splendor. Cut and uncut silk velvets, real gold threads in most elaborate patterns, brocatelles and damasks, as well as tapestries and needlework in brilliant hues were used by the affluent. There were handwoven linens and laces and all women of high position learned and practiced every form of fine needle-

First half of sixteenth century chest from the Ile de France
(Château O'Azay le Rideau)

work. In addition to the incomparable stained glass used in the church windows, there were glass vessels for use in the richer households, and pewter ones for the less wealthy. There was also faïence for jugs and household articles.

Henri II cabinet in two parts with marble inserts; second half of the sixteenth century

First half of sixteenth century cupboard

The French Renaissance was ushered in with the reign of François I, who succeeded to the throne of Louis XII in 1515, and moved the French court, which had been established in the Loire region for over a century, to Fontainebleau. The architects, painters, sculptors, furniture makers, and ornamentalists employed at Fontainebleau, many of whom were Italian, were greatly influenced by Italian art and borrowed their forms and decorations from the already highly developed Italian Renaissance. Their work, in what became known as the "School of Fontainebleau," had a long-range effect on the French art which followed, although interpretations varied in different sections. It is sometimes difficult to distinguish furniture of the François I period from Italian pieces of the same time, as both utilized the same leaf motifs, busts, and pilasters decorated with arabesques and grotesques.

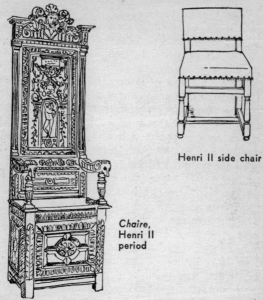

Henri II side chair

Chaire,
Henri II
period

In the reign of François I's son, Henri II, a very definite and beautiful furniture style evolved at Fontainebleau. Columns, tapering slightly at the top and bottom, formed the legs of fine chairs of simple design and were used brilliantly for table bases. Although apparently simple in line, these pieces of furniture were very subtly designed, often with inlaid woods and marble insets, and are of exquisite proportions. Some examples are still found from time to time on the open market.

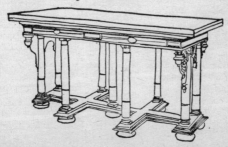

Late sixteenth century refectory table (Musée des Arts decoratifs)

Buffets of the early French Renaissance followed the old form of cupboards and were supported on a base with columns at the corners, decorated with medallions which often enclosed human heads, and with elaborately carved arabesques in very low relief. Tables of the Henri II period were higher than those of later date, and many had two, highly-carved console ends, connected by a stretcher near the bottom and an apron supporting a thick walnut extension top. Some of the most beautiful refectory tables had nine column supports and double tops which could be drawn out and extended at either end. Oak was largely abandoned for walnut and the *armoire a deux corps* (cupboard in two parts) came into existence at this time. The lower half, which formerly had served only as a support for the top, was now utilized as another cupboard, usually slightly larger than the upper one.

Jacques Androuet, known as **Du Cerceau** (1512–34), was an architect, draftsman and ornamentalist who had studied in Italy under Bramante. His *Receuil Grave de Meubles,* which was published in 1550, launched a new aesthetic approach, inspired by the antique, not only in elements of ornamentation, but also in rules of proportions and of logic in the choice of forms. Du Cerceau was the originator of the style of using long lateral columns, rising from the bottom of a cabinet to its top and created buffets and other furniture of unsurpassed beauty.

Another development in France, known as the "School of Burgundy," was greatly influenced by the art of the Low Countries. The work of **Hugues Sambin,** an architect, sculptor and cabinetmaker, who flourished in Dijon between 1549 and 1572, is typical of this school. Sambin's furniture was characterized by the use of bold human figures and by surfaces completely covered with carving.

At the end of the sixteenth century the style of architectural perspective in furniture was adopted, along with sculpture in low relief and incrustations of various types. Regional furniture styles fused and a single formula applied to the art of the whole of France.

Jean Goujon who was born about 1515, was one of the most celebrated sculptors of the French Renaissance. He worked for many years on the decoration of the Louvre and in 1550 went to Anet where he embellished the

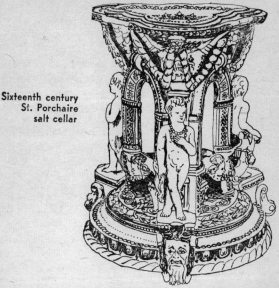

Sixteenth century
St. Porchaire
salt cellar

château of Diane de Poitiers. His famous statue of "Diana the Huntress" which was made for the courtyard of the château, is now in the Musée du Louvre, and a street in Paris bears his illustrious name.

Very fine enameled copperware was produced in Limoges from about 1530 until 1577 by such great artists as **Leonard Limosin,** who is known for his portraits; **Suzanne Court,** who created fabulously delicate salts; **Jean Court, Pierre Courteys,** and **Pierre Reymond,** who made religious plaques, small caskets and other precious articles in this medium.

The first mention of a glass mirror in France was made in the middle of the thirteenth century, although they are known to have existed as early as the Roman era. The mirror belonging to Diane de Poitiers is one of the earliest Renaissance mirrors to be identified and conserved. The first mirrors were approximately the size of a saucer and many of the earliest were hand mirrors. These, being precious, were set into frames of great beauty and of costly materials and workmanship.

Louis XIII chair with
period moquette

The luxuries of François I's time were increased and
perfected under his son Henri II, so we find items of
greater comfort appearing during his reign. Henri II was
succeeded by his sons Henri III, Henry IV, and finally by
Louis XIII, during whose reign a new style of furniture
came into existence. It was less stiff, more comfortable,
and more informal. Chairs had turned and twisted walnut
arms, stretchers and supports began to appear and panels

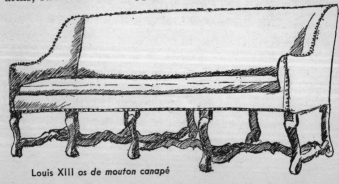

Louis XIII os de mouton canapé

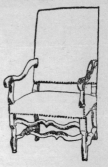

Louis XIII os de mouton
(mutton bone) armchair

Louis XIII ebony cabinet

on cabinets were often simpler with well-proportioned moldings as their only decorations.

The first real upholstery of chairs was begun in this period and replaced the heavy and very hard pillows which had formerly been used and moved from chair to chair as required; also, velvet replaced leather for the stretchers of folding, X-shaped stools. Wool upholstery fabrics were much in use during the reign of Henri II and were further popularized in the Henri IV and Louis XIII periods. These fabrics, which in France are called *moquettes,* were known throughout Europe as *velours d'Utrecht* after the Dutch city of Utrecht which was among the earliest to manufacture them. While their texture and design differed somewhat from the French product, they were not unlike it in appearance. The early French moquette is most often of a small design in many colors; the Dutch frequently in a single tone, with a larger stamped pattern. Thus chairs and settees became not only colorful, through the use of these brilliantly striking materials, but also cozier and more inviting in the cold and damp climate of northern Europe.

Early seventeenth
century
ebony cabinet

The magnificent tapestries which covered the stone walls of Gothic and Renaissance castles were soon supplemented by wool velvets, silk velvets, and brocatelles, thus giving additional warmth and protection from draughts. Bed curtains, covers, tablecloths and other fabrics played a most important part in interiors. Henri IV was so interested in the production of silk that he cultivated silkworms at his Château de Nerac. Later, planting mulberry trees in the Tuileries gardens, he engaged two hundred textile workers and built a very handsome edifice on a great square which was a part of his Palais de Tournelles. Over the opposition of his minister Sully, Henri IV pensioned these workers from his privy purse.

During the reign of Louis XIII, Cardinal Mazarin (1602–61) who was a great lover and patron of the arts, gave impetus to the advancement of decoration and his own palace is said to have been the finest in Europe. It was around this time that family portraits, as well as those of great men and the nobility, became familiar decoration in the houses of the well-to-do. Candlesticks and chandeliers, which in the earlier periods had generally been of wrought iron, bronze or *dinanderie* (or bell metal), and perhaps silver in the churches, now appeared in brass and pewter. Except in the churches and the houses of nobles,

Early fifteenth century gold enameled and jeweled figure of St. Catherine of Alexandria (Metropolitan Museum of Art)

Sixteenth century dinanderie candlesticks

chandeliers were scarce in France until the eighteenth century and people depended on candlesticks and wall sconces. Lighting was generally very dim and inadequate, and wax candles were so exorbitantly expensive that only the very rich could afford them. Others had to make do with malodorous tallow.

While contemplating the splendor of the artistic accomplishments in France, one might dream nostalgically of the beauty and elegance of life in that country from the Renaissance to the Revolution, and fail to take into account that the surroundings which delight our senses today were accompanied by acute discomfort and suffering for those living there at the time. The huge mantelpieces of the Renaissance, which were devised as an ornamental feature opposite the entrance door of a great hall, produced more draughts than heat. The rooms were always filled with smoke, making eyes water and tormenting succeeding generations. No one seemed able to cope with the problem efficiently and, lacking matches, people were obliged to keep their fires going throughout the year, even if only to sustain the glowing embers. According to Henri Havard, a famous nineteenth century author, writing on

Chasse, reliquary of the thirteenth century, of gilded bronze, gilded copper and rock crystal (Metropolitan Museum of Art)

conditions in France in the preceding century, relighting a dead fire was a major enterprise.

After two centuries of studying the problem of heat and smoke, it was finally solved to a certain extent in the seventeenth century by **Robert de Cotte,** nephew of the architect **Jules Hardouin Mansart.** De Cotte reduced the size of the flue and the opening of the fireplace, lowered the

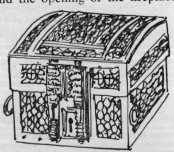

Fifteenth century wrought iron box for a *Livre d'Heures,* a Book of Hours.

whole structure, and was the first to place a mantelshelf above the opening, allowing for a mantel garniture and a mirror above it.

The receptions which the kings and queens held in their beds and which seem to us such a strange way to receive courtiers, were originally an expedient for keeping warm.

Fourteenth century *cuivre doré* (gilded copper) figure holding a reliquary; Decorated with enamel and glass (Metropolitan Museum of Art)

Louis XIV, called the "greatest sovereign on earth," suffered cruelly from the cold and the ills which accompanied it. His mistress, Mme. de Maintenon, had a sort of niche made for herself with upholstery fabrics on three sides to keep out the cold, for she found that even her sudden elevation to a high position as the king's mistress, did not guarantee her against rheumatism. Princes and princesses, fully dressed, received their friends in bed.

Louis XIV, known as the *Roi Soleil* or the Sun King, was the personification of luxury and grandeur. A radiating sun became his symbol and was incorporated into many designs in bronze and other decorations during his reign. Retaining his father's (Louis XIII) hunting lodge

Louis XIV velvet covered
bed with canopy

as the center, he built the Palais de Versailles around it, adding on both sides. Between the years 1661 and 1668, Le Vau was his architect. In 1668 further additions were undertaken which were far from completion when Le Vau died died in 1670. These were then carried on by Dorbay until 1678. But by then the insatiable and indefatigable King again had new plans for enlarging the already vast château. For this third change he enlisted the services of Jules Hardouin Mansart who undertook the vast project between 1678 and 1714.

The famous gardens and fountains of Versailles were originally planned by Le Nôtre but throughout the entire reign of Louis XIV work was continued uninterruptedly by various others. Neither the château nor the gardens were ever considered complete and throughout his reign workmen swarmed over Versailles, to the great discomfort of the nobles and many courtiers who preferred to endure almost anything rather than absent themselves from the close proximity to their sovereign.

The Louis XIV period was, like most moments of great prosperity, full of rivalry and jealousy. Each wanted to outdo his neighbor in elegance and splendor. France led the world, and every vain man or woman wanted to lead France. As an illustration of the atmosphere of the time, I might cite the case of Louis XIV's Minister of Finance, Nicolas Fouquet, who entertained the whole French court at his beautiful Château de Vaux-le-Vicomte with such ostentatious extravagance that it aroused suspicion concerning the origin of his great wealth. Upon investigation it was discovered that he had built and furnished his coveted château with the funds entrusted to him by his sovereign and the state. He was condemned to prison in Pignerolo (Piedmont), where he died in 1680.

The introduction of foreign furniture into France by the Italian Cardinal Mazarin, had been followed by an influx of foreign workmen from Italy and the Low Countries. Among these were the bronze-makers Cucci, and Caffieri who became the founder of a long and distinguished line

Louis XIV gilded wood console table

of French craftsmen. By the time the ill-fated Fouquet had built his château of Vaux-le-Vicomte, there was a group of French workmen who had learned the foreign techniques. Immediately after Fouquet's arrest in 1659, the king took possession of the tapestry works which the fallen minister had established at Maincy and to which all the best craftsmen working at Vaux-le-Vicomte had been attached. Louis XIV moved the Maincy works to Gobelins on the outskirts of Paris and established there the *Manufacture Royale des Meubles de la Couronne*.

The centralization of state-supported artisans for the production of the luxury arts owed its success in large degree to its first director, Charles LeBrun, in whom Fouquet had recognized great ability and whom he had appointed director of works at Vaux. LeBrun's personal achievements were extraordinary. Nothing at Gobelins was undertaken before 1685 except under his personal supervision, and during that period he himself provided the major number of designs for tapestry, furniture, sculpture, and architectural decoration, including goldsmith's work and conveyances, while also acting as *Premier Peintre du Roi* and director of buildings. The construction of the famous *Galerie des Glaces* at Versailles was begun under his direction in 1678 and completed in 1683, the year after Louis XIV took up residence in the palace.

The motive for the establishment of Gobelins was not merely a desire to create things of unsurpassed beauty, but also an attempt to raise the standard of the luxury arts in France and to secure her economic and moral ascendancy in Europe. Due to certain regulations favoring the training of the children of the workmen of the Gobelin factory, these gradually replaced the foreigners who had been much in evidence at its inception.

Before the reign of Louis XIV there had been no real court in the sense of that now gathered at Versailles where the love of luxury and ostentation created a feverish rivalry among the courtiers. The insatiable desire to enlarge, improve, and do over whatever had been done by a predecessor caused the destruction of many beautiful interiors and the dispersal of their furnishings. Seen from the vantage point of the twentieth century, this fury of artistic expression had its great drawbacks, for it left very few palaces exactly as they had been conceived by the builders. One is disappointed, more often than not, in visiting châteaux to find that they have been altered and despoiled of their original treasures. Happily however, a great effort is now being made to restore Versailles to its former appearance and as many pieces of its original furniture as possible are being brought back.

The attitude of the nobles in the Louis XIV period was

in some respects very similar to that of the rich today, in that as soon as a man has more of this world's goods than he requires to keep body and soul together, he begins to surround himself with beauty, and aspires to do so with more taste and discrimination than his neighbor. What can be more delightful for a successful man of affairs than to see his artistic acumen justified by the rising value of pieces similar to those he himself has collected and to know that his patronage has encouraged high artistic standards.

Louis XIV
Boulle commode

During the reign of Louis XIV, furniture and decorations took on more magnificence, and the regal style required by the new splendor blossomed out under the artistry of such men as the furniture maker André-Charles Boulle and the *bronzier,* Jean-Jacques Caffieri. There are few pieces of furniture extant which are indisputably by the hand of Boulle, but the style is well known to even the average layman. Intricate brass designs inlaid in a veneer of tortoise shell or ebony, rendered even more splendid by the addition of heavy gilded bronze mounts, are typical of his style.

A sheet of brass and a sheet of tortoise shell were glued together and the design was cut into both simultaneously, thus producing two identical pieces. The brass was then imbedded in a background of tortoise shell and the piece of furniture decorated in this manner was designated as having been made *en première parti,* whereas the piece on which the tortoise shell was affixed to a brass background, was known as *en contre parti*. Thus a pair of objects was made with identical decorations, in reverse. Today very few such pairs exist. but Boulle pieces *en première parti*

Cupboard in the
style of
Charles-André Boulle

are considered far more desirable than those *en contre parti* for they are more brilliant and have a richer and more pleasing effect. Such fame and popularity was attached to the name of Boulle that his style was much imitated in the nineteenth century and anything with a tortoise shell ground and brass inlay became known as "Buhl" irrespective of date or place of origin.

It was in this period that the *fauteuil* or *canapé à châssis* was devised in which upholstery fabric covered a wooden framework which slipped into the frame of the piece. This expedient made it possible to change the decoration of a room according to the seasons and in the more sumptuous palaces there were as many as four changes of upholstery. Heavily embroidered or brocaded fabrics were used in winter, with lighter colors and materials for spring and summer. The *cabriole* or curved leg, made its appearance around this time, but was less accentuated than it became later during the reign of Louis XV.

Although the long reign of Louis XIV is known as Le Grand Siècle, or the great century, the King was involved in very frustrating and expensive wars which, along with his great extravagance in building, led to a very much embarrassed exchequer. He was obliged to raise more and more money to pay for the wars, so that in 1689 he resorted to the expedient of melting down much, if not all, of the existing silver plate and ornaments. In 1699 he issued another edict ordering the melting of gold and silver vessels, and in 1709, a third. For this reason there is a great dearth of seventeenth and early eighteenth-century French silver on the market today. In 1759, during the Seven Years War, silver plate was again confiscated and melted down, so that Louis XV silver is also very scarce. Today, seventeenth and eighteenth-century silver is very highly prized and whatever escaped the melting pot commands an extremely high price.

The destruction of the silver used by the nobles and great families encouraged men such as Meissonnier and Caffieri to rival its beauty with marvels of imagination in gilded bronze. It was also the incentive which activated the many faïence factories which sprang up to create substitutes for household articles of which the upper classes had been deprived. However, the nobility, not completely satisfied with the output of the ceramic industry, turned to the enamels of Limoges for the very elaborate and luxurious pictorial pieces it desired. At Limoges they were producing brilliant enameled copper ornaments and table decorations, including precious "salts." This preference of

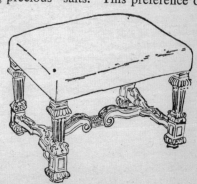

Louis XIV stool

the French aristocrats for enamels retarded somewhat the acceptance of faïence on the upper levels of French taste.

The floors at Versailles were originally of varicolored marble squares, but around the Régence and early Louis XV periods, these were changed to interlaced hardwood in a special pattern. This type of floor set the style for other princely châteaux to follow and has come to be known as *parquet à la Versailles*. Over the floors, but not quite covering them, was a woven wool rug. Frequently with a black background and always very elaborate in design, these rugs often bore the emblem of the king or prince for whom they were made. In the Louis XIV period the Savonnerie rug added splendor and warmth to an already magnificent setting.

Seventeenth century Savonnerie wool rug with black background

CHAPTER THREE

Régence and Louis XV

The rectangular wall panels and heavy cornices characteristic of the classical style of Louis XIV, began to be
replaced around 1700 by a new and lighter style of
decoration. The architect **Robert de Cotte** and the sculptor,
engraver and designer. **Jean Bérain**, as well as **Pierre
Lepautre** and others, began to introduce humorous and
whimsical designs, with delicate arabesque and carvings of
birds and leaves in low relief which often overran the
frames of panels. Monkeys in the role of human beings
were also introduced at this time as Bérain and de Cotte
gained ascendancy over the style at court.

Régence carved and gilded oak console table

This phase of French art developed into what is known as the *Régence* style. Although the Duke of Orléans only acted as Regent for the young Louis XV between 1715

Régence carved oak table

and 1723, the transition in style between the Louis XIV and the Louis XV periods took its name from that short interim. No style begins or ends abruptly; it is felt years before and carries over into the succeeding reign or period. Objects in the Louis XIV style continued to be made until 1720, while the first stirrings of the Régence style were felt as early as 1700. Similarly, Louis XV style furniture began to appear as early as 1725, while the Régence continued to be made as late as 1730.

Juste-Aurèle Meissonnier (1695-1750), who became "Designer to the King" in 1725, a post formerly held by Jean Bérain, was the father of the Rococo style, which swept across the French border into Germany, Austria, and

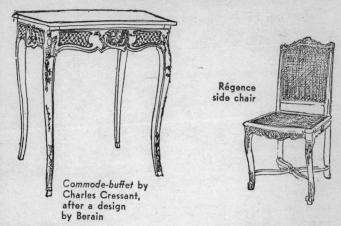

Commode-buffet by
Charles Cressant,
after a design
by Berain

Régence
side chair

Italy. His books of engravings called *Oeuvres* showed
boundless imagination in the design of rocaille forms. In
Germany the hard paste porcelain of Meissen and Nymph-
enburg lent itself especially to the asymmetrical treatment
of his *rocaille* designs, which were based on shell, vegetable and animal forms.

After the marriage of Louis XIV to Mme. de Maintenon, there was an easing of the pomp and protocol at
court and a tendency to unbend toward greater ease and
comfort. The sequence of the changes in the spirit of the
times is reflected and can be followed step by step through

Régence
carved oak
bed

Régence console table after a design by Meissonier

the development and construction of the chairs made during the transition. From the straight, rigid, high-backed, formal chairs of Louis XIV's time, small differences began to appear. The first of these was that the arms, always heretofore rising directly over the front legs, were placed further back, and the legs reduced in height, allowing for greater ease. Many have attributed the new position of the arms to the style in women's dresses, but as the pannier only appeared in 1717 and a *fauteuil* with arms considerably behind the termination of the leg is known as early as 1685, this explanation is hardly valid.

Besides being lower, the legs were slightly curved and elaborately carved, as was the woodwork of the frame

Regence armchair
with stretcher

Régence carved and gilded armchair

under the seat, which now showed instead of being covered by upholstery. The shell motif was much in evidence and legs frequently terminated in small cloven hoofs. Gradually the height of the backs, too, was reduced and

Régence carved and gilded *dossier plat* armchair

Louis XV side chair by Boulard

a gentle curve appeared in place of the rectangular lines of the earlier periods. The next change was that the wood on the back of the chair, which previously had been covered by upholstery, was now visible. There was an increasing curve in the legs, and feet terminated in scrolls, under which were small hexagonal bases, now almost all consumed by wear. The x-shaped stretchers between the legs,

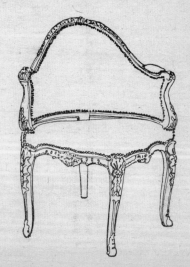

Régence
fauteuil de bureau

Louis XV armchair by Foliot, circa 1770

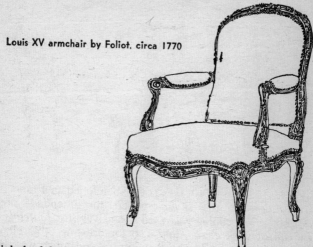

which had been so prevalent during the Louis XIV and early Régence periods, began to disappear around 1720 to 1725, as chairs became lighter and the need ceased to exist. Upholstered armpads appeared after the Régence.

Most chairs were either painted, gilded or silvered. The latter type, which reached the height of its popularity

Régence carved and gilded
fauteuil à chassis

Louis XV *canapé a corbeille*

around 1730 to 1740, was soon abandoned in France, as oxidization of the silver spoiled the intended effect. Around 1740 caning was used extensively for *fauteuils de bureau* or desk chairs, and also for dressing table chairs. Except for these odd chairs, natural wood finish was used much less frequently in the Louis XV period than we are led to believe today, seeing as we do, so much furniture that has been stripped of its paint. A great deal of this *décapage* was undoubtedly necessary after two centuries of wear and probably even of repainting. However, all these changes came gradually and differed according to the cabinetmaker and his ideas and preferences.

The Louis XV style which evolved is considered more feminine and graceful than what went before. And while the changed position of the arms of the chairs is probably

Louis XV *lit de repos à crosse*

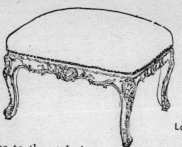

Louis XV gilded stool

not due to the style in women's dresses, it did inspire the creation of a new form of chair, called a *marquise:* a broad chair or small *canapé* especially built to accommodate the wide skirts and panniers of the Louis XV period.

Canapés (or sofas), and *lits de repos* (or day-beds) were innovations which followed the trend toward greater ease. The importance attached to comfort and the new role of women increasingly affected styles in decoration and the forms of furniture. *Bergères* which came into existence around 1725, and which are still held in the highest esteem, are large, deep, closed-arm chairs which embrace the body in a relaxed position rather than in the formal posture which etiquette had demanded a century before.

In the Louis XV period, it was considered a great privilege and sign of high rank to be permitted to sit on a stool in the presence of the King. This occasioned great intrigues and jealousies among the nobles and resulted in quarrels and scandals over a period of several centuries. Stools were always a very important feature of the decoration, and today, when they are extremely scarce, they are highly prized and lend great charm and style to a period interior.

Louis XV stool

Louis XV *dos d'âne* desk
with *marquetrie à fleurs*

The Louis XV period abounded in new forms of furniture and pieces which had never been imagined before. The *bureau plat* or table desk, already known in the Louis XIV period, became an important element in a room. Then the *bureau en dos d'âne* or drop-leaf desk appeared (the French name describes its shape as that of an ass's back), which led to the upright *secrétaire* with its drop-front and marquetry decoration. A tall, narrow chest of drawers, called a *semainier,* because of its seven drawers, supposedly one for each day of the week, also was introduced at this time. *Semainiers* ranged from very elabor-

Louis XV *secrétaire* with
marquetrie à fleurs

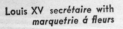

ately decorated marquetry pieces with marble tops, to modest walnut or fruitwood in the provinces. The type is similar to what has been known in America for generations, as a *chiffonier,* although the American product is larger, wider, and has no specific number of drawers.

Bedside tables called *tables de chevet* were very similar to those known as *en-cas* (in case). Both had drawers under their marble tops and little cupboards below. The commode, or chest of drawers, which had first been seen at the end of the reign of Louis XIV, became one of the most characteristic pieces of Louis XV furniture. The first commodes were made with three drawers, or with two large and two smaller ones above them. Their bow fronts were ornamented with bronze escutcheons and drawer-pulls and the corners and feet were protected by decorative bronze *chutes* and *sabots.* At first these commodes were heavy and their legs short, so that the lowest drawer was only a few inches from the floor. These are known today as *commodes en tombeaux.* The marble tops varied

Louis XV
natural wood commode

in type according to the coloring of the woods used but always followed the curved outlines of the piece. As time went on, commodes grew lighter in appearance and higher on their legs, with three drawers changing to two. The latter are more suitable in a drawing room today, while the three drawer variety is more practical in a bedroom

The finest commodes of the Louis XV and Louis XVI periods have no dividing strip between the upper and lower drawers. Instead, the front panel is treated as a single unit with no obvious constructional consideration of its utility. When closed, it shows no sign of functioning as

Louis XV two drawer
marquetry commode by L. Boudin

two separate drawers, while the bronzes heighten the illu-
sion that the front is one solid panel. The drawer pulls are
often bronze scrolls and form a part of the general design.

Formal dining rooms did not exist, as such, in the Louis
XV period. Anterooms were used for that purpose and
tables set up almost anywhere that seemed appropriate
or convenient at the time. In winter it might have been
close to a fire; in summer on a terrace. When serving many
people a wooden plank was placed on sawhorses and
covered with a long tablecloth. No special dining table was
made until the Louis XVI period, so that now when

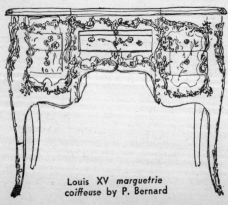

Louis XV *marquetrie*
coiffeuse by P. Bernard

people desire to furnish a dining room completely in the Louis XV style, they are obliged to have a table made to order. This rarely turns out well for there seems to be something incongruous in a Louis XV style table of a size and proportion required in a modern dining room.

Tables à coiffer or dressing tables were first made at this time. A center sliding panel enclosed a mirror which had deep wells on either side with a slide in the center and a drawer below. The lefthand well was frequently equipped with a variety of fine porcelain jars for rouge, ointments and toilet preparations considered essential in an age when water was used most sparingly. There were also silver-topped perfume bottles and many other items deemed necessary to the achievement of a lady's charming appearance. Wash basins and ewers of fabulous beauty are still to be found in soft paste Sèvres porcelain, and Marie Antoinette's exquisite rock crystal set is in the Musée du Louvre in Paris. These will startle a twentieth century observer as much for their small dimensions as for their extraordinary beauty.

Mme. du Barry was known to have taken a cold dip every morning, much to the amazement of her contemporaries. Some have suggested that this habit gave her such unusual freshness that Louis XV was attracted to her.

Louis XV *trictrac* (backgammon table)

The enormous vogue for indoor games during the reign of Louis XV created a demand for tables for that purpose. Some were square, some rectangular, some triangular and later some were round, all according to the requirements of the game for which they were designed. They usually had a drawer or drawers, or a well for the counters used in the game. They frequently had indented candlestick holders and many tables folded, forming three-cornered consoles with rounded corners. The playing surface was usually covered in green baize or needlework. By the middle of the eighteenth century trictrac (backgammon) tables and checker-top tables were made for chess and checkers, generally with removable tops.

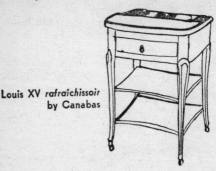

Louis XV *rafraîchissoir* **by Canabas**

The *servante or rafraîchissoir,* as it is more frequently called, also appeared at this time. This was a rectangular table on casters, with rounded corners and a marble top fitted with two silver-plated receptacles in which to chill

Louis XV marquetry *liseuse*   **Louis XV small lacquer** *dos d'âne* **desk**

Louis XV marquetry table desk
by Migeon and Dubois

bottles. There was a drawer for cutlery and napkins and one or two undershelves. Canabas designed some especially charming *rafraîchissoirs* in solid mahogany: Louis XV is known to have ordered one for his own use in 1735, for this table freed him from the constant presence of servants in attendance and perfectly suited his desire for privacy.

The greatest possible care and imagination were lavished on the production of little tables, which are still amongst the most highly prized pieces of furniture produced in the eighteenth century. These tiny tables which play such an important role in the furnishing of a French room of this period have marquetry or marble tops; others have Sèvres porcelain tops especially made for the purpose. They have small drawers either in the front or on the sides or pull-out *tirettes* (extensions). Some have solid

Louis XV *bureau plat* (flat top desk)

little doors, others have sliding doors; some are like small commodes, while others have undershelves. The one thing they all have in common is that they are finished on all sides and the back so they can stand free in a room and be seen from all angles. Frequently, despite their diminutive size, they have compartments in the drawers for inkpots and writing equipment.

Louis XV *table à ouvrage*
by Delorme

Louis XV small table with undershelf

Little tables of high quality are increasingly scarce, and it is almost true that the smaller the table, the more it will cost. One of the great spurs to the art of cabinet-making in France in the Louis XV period was the guild, or *Corporation des Menuisiers-Ébénistes* which protected its artisans by controls on competition and encouraged them to remain active and to train their children to succeed them. The *maître-menuisiers* and *maître-ébénistes* could practice their painstaking and time-consuming occupations with serenity, secure in the knowledge that they could not be crushed by the more aggressive or unscrupulous in the profession, and could allow their creative genius to develop without the hampering financial worries that normally beset artists of all kinds.

Although there were no guild regulations or laws prohibiting a man from working in more than one branch of furniture making, they rarely encroached on each other's fields. A *menuisier* was a craftsman who made chairs, beds, chaise longes, stools and what some call "seat furniture." He also made consoles and the furniture which was part of the room. He worked in solid wood which was carved and later stained, painted or gilded.

An *ébéniste* on the other hand, was one who made veneered furniture such as commodes, tables, and book-cases. Still others specialized in clock cases and very intricate pictorial marquetry and the decoration of boxes and miscellaneous small pieces.

A high degree of proficiency was maintained by the guild and after an apprenticeship of many years, each prospective *maître* had to prove his ability by making an especially fine piece of furniture to be judged by a committee. If successful, the applicant was then obliged to pay a very large entrance fee. A *maître* was permitted to have several *compagnons,* or assistants; obliged to have one apprentice at all times; and had the right to teach his own children or nephews without restriction; for sons and sons-in-law of a master took precedence over all others, and their entrance fee was only nominal. Similarly, a workman who married the widow of a *maître,* and even the widow herself, if she was assisted by a capable craftsman, had the right to maintain the workshop of her deceased husband.

In addition to the members of the guild, the king could create *maîtres* of his own choosing. These extremely able craftsmen who were known as *artisans privilégés* or *ouvriers de la couronne,* were free of guild restrictions, beyond its jurisdiction and not subject to the usual taxes. They were granted special protection and given workshops in buildings belonging to the Crown, such as the Louvre, the Arsenal, parts of the Temple, or the Gobelins. As most of the work of these artisans was ordered by the Crown, it was unsigned.

Other free artisans who were not members of the guild, sought refuge in places where medieval rights still existed, such as the Abbey of Saint-Antoine des Champs and the Temple. French workmen had gone to the small courts of the electoral princes of Germany during the Louis XIV period and German artisans had learned furniture making from them. Later many German craftsmen came to France in the hope of finding greater scope and remuneration for their work, and promptly found employment with French masters, whose tastes and styles they absorbed while saving enough money to become independent. They then took advantage of the privileges of the faubourg Saint-Antoine to establish businesses of their own. Oeben, Riesener, Weisweiler and Beneman, for example, began in this way.

To combat competition from outside the guild, a law was passed in 1741 making it mandatory for each craftsman to sign his product. The mark was worked in relief on a bar of lead and a hammer blow imprinted it on the back, underside, or upright corner of a piece of furniture. Each mark was registered at a central office, which added a stamp of control formed of three letters, "J.M.E." standing for *Jurande* or *Juré des Menuisiers Ébénists*. Fraudulent use of a mark was severely punished and all unsigned pieces were automatically considered contraband and were subject to a fine of twenty livres.

Not all signatures found today are clear or decipherable however. Some are the remnants of marks placed by the dealer in raw wood and others are those of the dealer who sold the piece. Nothing made before the Louis XV period was ever signed and much fine furniture made on special order was delivered directly from shop to client and so never passed through the central office. Furniture for the Crown was marked only with the initials of the palace and possibly of the room for which it was intended. In addition, some dealers, jealously guarding the sources of their finest wares, removed signatures in order to prevent others from contacting the makers directly.

Not all signatures are genuine, and it is far more important that a piece be authentic than for it to be signed. False signatures have often been affixed to mediocre or poor pieces, as well as to clever forgeries. When the style is in accord with the signature of the man who is supposed to have made it, one can assume that the signature is authentic. With practice, the collector becomes familiar with a cabinetmaker's style, and if the piece of furniture is genuinely of the period, the lack of a signature should not

Eighteenth century gilt bronze *appliques* with animals

be an obstacle, although it is only natural, when buying a fine piece, to be pleased to know the maker's name.

In addition to the *Corporation des Menuisiers-Ébénistes,* there were other guilds connected with the production of fine furniture. The bronze *fondeurs* or casters; the *ciseleurs,* engravers and chasers; and the *doreurs* or gilders; produced *bronze d'ameublement* which included the bronze mounts and hardware for wooden pieces of furniture, as well as sconces, andirons, clock cases and all the hardware required on doors and windows. The organization of these guilds was similar to that of the *Menuisier-Ébénistes*

Louis XV gilt bronze *chinoiserie appliques*

and these workmen àlso had to submit a specimen of their work to the committee for approval before they could acquire the status of *maître*. In 1776 these groups joined

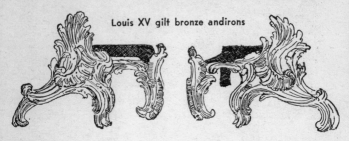

Louis XV gilt bronze andirons

into a single guild. Some fine pieces of gilded bronze have a tiny mark in the form of the letter "C" surmounted by a crown, stamped into the bronze in some inconspicuous spot. For a time it was thought to be the signature of Caffieri, but this has been proved incorrect. The most recent theory is that it was either the mark of a specific group of gilders between the years 1745 and 1749, or possibly a control mark required by law during that brief

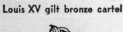

Louis XV gilt bronze cartel

Regence mirror

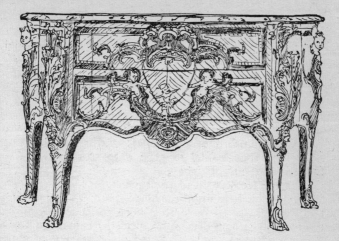

Régence commode by Charles Cressent

period. In any case it is extremely pleasant to find, as it dates the piece quite accurately.

The light colored walls enhanced by gilding, which the architect Oppenord created for the Regent early in the eighteenth century, called for a new approach, and the charming heads and arabesques of Watteau inspired decoration and furniture mounts. The youthful Charles Cressent (1685–1768), after working briefly in the Boulle style, felt the new trend for lighter and more graceful furniture and became the most representative cabinetmaker of the Régence and early Louis XV periods. Serpentine fronts, splayed sides and multicolored woods used in the marquetry, as well as asymmetrical gilded bronze

Louis XIV Boulle commode

rocaille mounts were typical characteristics. The Régence style is considered to have lasted until 1730, after which the dignity which had been the heritage of the preceding generations gave way to gaiety and frivolity. Grace and freedom of movement became the new keynotes, sought in all decorative fields.

As glassmakers acquired the ability to make mirrors of large dimensions, these became important decorative adjuncts and were incorporated into many designs for wall paneling. Gilt bronze chandeliers and girandoles were hung with rock crystal or glass drops cut so that their facets would reflect light and produce a brilliant effect, despite the feeble light of the candles.

While gilded furniture remained the ultimate in luxury and was considered the correct thing for state and formal salons, polychrome decoration of chairs came into vogue and was extremely popular for all other rooms during the reign of Louis XV. The strong reds, yellows and sapphire blues of the late Louis XIV period continued to be used during the early years of his grandson's reign, but little by little, colors grew more delicate and were planned to harmonize with the upholstery silks used with them. Even

Louis XVI black lacquer
bonheur du jour
by C. C. Saunier

on gilded chairs, garlands of flowers were painted in naturalistic colors designed to bring out the carving. Around 1755–1760 white paint without the addition of any other color was used more and more. Chairs ordered for the Petit Trianon, although still completely in the Louis XV style, were painted *blanc de plomb* or lead white. This is the same color which, after use, dust and what is known as the patina of time, became known as *gris* (gray) *Trianon*.

Oriental forms and lacquer became extremely fashionable and commodes of this material were and still are, considered the height of elegance and beauty. Lacquered pieces were first made with imported Chinese and Japanese panels, which were mostly in the form of screens, chests or oriental furniture, which in their original form, did not find favor in Europe. The eighteenth-century lacquered furniture which has come down to us is of several different types. The ébénistes of the Louis XV period generally chose Chinese lacquer with gold and colored decoration, with red predominating, usually on a black ground. Less frequently, the background was red. Other background colors, such as green and ivory, are very rarely seen and are very likely French workmanship in imitation of the Chinese. The cabinetmakers of the Louis XVI period showed a preference for Japanese lacquer, which harmonizes particularly well with the restraint and finesse of the furniture of that style. The ground is also black, but the decoration is gold and silver, sometimes in relief, without any color. The designs are smaller and more delicate and of the finest imaginable execution. There is none of the boldness found in what is known as "Coromandel" lacquer, which was a product of the province of Ho Nan in central China. This rare and beautiful lacquer used in the Louis XV period is very colorful and so thick that it can be engraved. The black background of a reddish tinge turns almost brown with age. Some of the Coromandel lacquers used for furniture date from the Ming period, equivalent to the late sixteenth century in our reckoning. These are extremely rare and desirable.

Since original oriental panels rarely if ever quite fitted the pieces they were destined to cover, the French cabinetmakers had to employ the greatest ingenuity to achieve the

Louis XV *Vernis Martin* commode

desired results. Gilded bronze mounts designed to frame panels that were too small, and other expedients were employed to produce masterpieces of furniture making. Since it was extremely difficult to veneer a commode—especially a Louis XV *bombé,* one with a swelled and curved front and sides—with a straight panel, the French craftsmen went to great lengths to learn to imitate the oriental technique of lacquering. Later, as the demand increased for these pieces, lacquer panels were ordered in the Orient in the standard sizes required by the French cabinetmakers. But lacquering is a very slow process and these panels made on order and in haste, are of an inferior quality. Between 1733 and 1740 the Duc de Bourbon organized a workshop at Chantilly where lacquer in the oriental style was made with such skill that even connoisseurs were deceived by it.

At this point the Martin brothers became prominent as a result of their mastery of the technique of lacquer on wood which is now universally known as *Vernis Martin.* It was used on furniture as well as for wall panels, sedan chairs, needlecases and memorandum tablets. Although the Martin brothers learned their technique from the oriental models they had seen and studied, their subjects were purely French, in the spirit of the eighteenth century.

One of the most whimsical and delightful practices of this period was the creation of decorations in the Chinese style, known as *chinoiserie*. Frequently very unlike the real Chinese people and scenes it depicted, *chinoiserie* was gay and jolly and full of imagination, as the French genius expressed itself with inimitable charm and color. In 1708 Watteau was engaged to decorate the Château de la Muette with *chinoiseries* based on authentic Chinese drawings, and in 1761 Marie Leczinska who was a very skillful amateur painter, had her own chamber redecorated to accommodate the *chinoiserie* panels she had painted.

Louis XV gilt bronze mounted Chinese porcelain *brûle parfum*

Louis XV gilt bronze mounted Chinese porcelain figure with Vincennes porcelain flowers

This passion for Chinese art is further illustrated by the tremendous vogue around the middle of the eighteenth century for Chinese porcelains mounted in gilded bronze by the best *ciseleurs* of the time. The day book of a famous jeweler or *marchand bijoutier,* named Lazare-Devaux, lists mounted Oriental porcelains as the source of half his income between the years 1748 and 1749. Duplessis, the brothers Slodtz, and various other masters were responsible for some of the finest of these pieces, a few of which can be seen in the great museums today. Some are now in public and private collections, but they are growing increasingly scarce and valuable.

As Meissen porcelain of quality was imported into France, gilded bronze mounts were often made to support groups and single figures. Candlesticks, decorated with birds and flowers, and many other articles, such as inkstands and clocks were elaborately mounted in France. Following the French fashion, some mounts were then made in Meissen itself, but neither the quality nor the design can compete with the French article.

The word *ébéniste* or cabinetmaker came into existence when very fine cabinet work was carried out in ebony. But after the reign of Louis XIV and when the great vogue for Boulle furniture was past, the desire for lighter colors and more varied furniture led the *ébénistes* to import all available exotic woods from the Far East and the Americas. Although they had a great variety at their disposal, they still resorted to tinting various colors not provided for by nature. A technical description in books of the period of how this was accomplished makes entertaining reading. Some of the lovely colors we so much admire were made with fresh manure.

Although Louis XV was much interested in architecture and indulged his love of building to an extent which proved a serious financial embarrassment to the state, he did not share Louis XIV's passion for decorating royal palaces. The tastes of Louis XV, dictated by a love of personal comfort and intimate surroundings, led him to abandon the use of the Grande Chambre de Louis XIV except for the ceremonies of *le levee* and *le coucher,* and to have a smaller bedchamber built in what had been the billiard room of Louis XIV.

The life of Louis XV at Versailles was spent increasingly in the Petits Appartements, where he could live the life of a private gentleman, entertaining his personal friends and devoting some of his spare time to scientific research, mechanical inventions and to his hobby of lathe turning, which at the time was a popular pastime.

He created several pieces of mechanical furniture for his personal use and a lift, called a *chaise volante* which he had installed at Versailles for Mme. de Châteauroux. He also ordered a *table volante* installed in the Petits Appartements at Trianon and in other châteaux. These tables sank through the floor to the kitchen quarters where they could be prepared with food and everything required for a meal, making it possible for the king to raise them again and enjoy complete privacy with his friends. *Meubles à transformations* as these mechanical pieces were called, were characteristic of the latter part of the Louis XV period. One marvels at the ingenuity demonstrated in making what seem to us to be quite uselessly versatile pieces. But during the reign of Louis XV Versailles became so tremendously over-crowded with nobles who wanted, at all costs, to be close to their sovereign, that rooms were at a premium and grew so small that even princes of the blood were lodged in tiny cell-like bedrooms. It is probably this condition, together with their taste for mechanical devices which inspired the cabinet-makers to produce furniture with two different uses, despite the fact that a piece usually looks better when it serves only one. Some of these pieces are miraculously beautiful, despite their double use, but frequently the lines are spoiled by the inclusion of a means of transformation.

The Marquis de Vendières, brother of Mme. de Pompadour (later created the Marquis de Marigny), was, through her influence, appointed Director of Buildings.

Bureau de Roi, the famous desk of Louis XV

From the end of 1749 until late in 1751 he prepared himself for that very high and responsible post by journeying through Italy with the architect Soufflot and the artist

Louis XV kidney shaped table
with *tambour* front by Bayer

Oval table, transition
between Louis XV
and Louis XVI

Charles Nicolas Cochin, the Younger. In 1758 Cochin published his *Observations on the Antiquities of Herculaneum,* which helped to spark the beginning of the Neoclassic style.

Mme. de Pompadour and the court were slow to evince interest in the new Greek and antique forms that suddenly made their appearance, and the Marquis de Marigny himself, showed little enthusiasm for the birth of the Louis XVI style. However the avant-garde of France's literary and artistic circles was interested in this return to classical forms as early as 1764, Lalive de Jully wrote that his house was furnished with pieces in the Greek taste and Cochin in his memoir, wrote that Louis de Lorraine (1713–59) had designed these decorations and was the first artist to bring the heavy swags, vases and garlands of the Louis XVI style into fashion.

One of the greatest ébénistes of the Louis XV period, Jean François Oeben, began the famous *"Bureau de Roi"* in 1760, which he had almost completed when he died in

1763. It was finished in 1769 by his assistant, Jean **Henri** Riesner, who probably executed the elaborate pictorial marquetry from the original Oeben design and **may** have added a few details of his own, as the *bureau* also contains neo-classic elements. Thus the styles of the Louis XV and XVI periods were being made simultaneously and many "transition pieces" had some characteristics of both. Late Louis XV pieces have relatively simple marquetry bodies, bronzes decorating only the outlines and functional use of the piece, and pictorial marquetry of **a** semi-classical character; thus forecasting the Louis XVI style.

CHAPTER FOUR

Transition
and
Louis XVI

The discovery of Herculaneum and Pompeii in 1748 sparked an interest in France in classical forms. When the German scholar Johann Joachim Winckelmann published his writings on Greek and Roman art from 1755 to 1764 and Cochin's *Observations on the Antiquities of Herculaneum* appeared in 1758, Paris was swept with enthusiasm for neo-classic forms.

Marie Antoinette, the daughter of Maria Theresa of Austria, married the Dauphin of France in the year 1770; four years after their marriage, Louis XV, the Dauphin's grandfather, died and Louis XVI succeeded to the throne. Because of the young queen's Austrian origin, many German craftsmen harbored high hopes of obtaining her favor and making a place for themselves in the French capital. In this they were not disappointed and a number of them, including Weisweiler and Beneman, were commissioned to work for the Crown.

By 1785 almost a third of the cabinetmakers in Paris were foreigners and their products were as desirable as those of the French. These men became a serious problem for the established members of the *Corporation des Menuisier-Ébénistes* which tried to force the newcomers to join the guild as quickly as possible. In order to abolish what it considered unfair competition, the guild reduced admission dues and allowed foreigners to pay them in ten installments. Naturalization restrictions were also relaxed at this time and Protestants, as well as Catholics, were allowed to become members of the guild. This in turn brought a new influx of young workmen from Germany, who were not yet acclimated when the Revolution began. Because of their youth and disorientation, these lads, mostly under twenty years of age, entered enthusiastically into the anarchy which ensued, and about sixty of them played a conspicuous part in the storming of the Bastille.

Riesener, who was already established in the late Oeben's workshop, began in the 1770's to simplify his marquetry and to make it more geometrical in character. Pictorial panels were generally centered in the front of a piece only and the rest decorated with a small over-all pattern. Riesener's prominence as a protegé of the queen, placed him in a most enviable position and others followed the trend he had established.

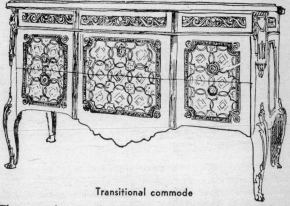

Transitional commode

The conspicuous changes in a Transition commode, are the rectangular carcase, the cut corners or stiles, and the legs which describe a more gentle curve than those of the Louis XV period; in fact, legs are almost straight on the inside and show only a very slight curve on the outside. Chairs sometimes had curved Louis XV backs and arms, but straight, or what is known as "console" legs. In other words, the chairs are neither Louis XV in design nor pure Louis XVI and are therefore known as Transition.

During that time and in the early Louis XVI period, new pieces of furniture began to appear.

One of these innovations was a *bonheur-du-jour,* a small upright desk, often elaborately inlaid, and supplied with a little cupboard or bookshelf at the back. Another was a jewel cabinet on high legs, with a drop-front enclosing small drawers in its interior.

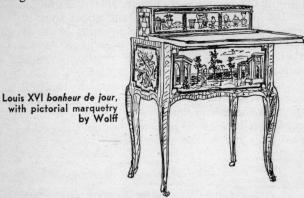

Louis XVI *bonheur de jour,* with pictorial marquetry by Wolff

Trictrac (or backgammon) tables, as well as card tables, had existed as early as the Régence, but there were relatively few compared with the quantities produced in the Louis XVI period. Usually made of mahogany, these

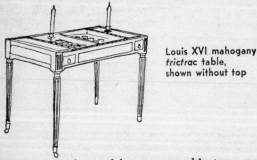

Louis XVI mahogany *trictrac* table, shown without top

tables are rectangular and have removable tops, one side of which is covered in leather, the other in baize. When the top is on, the table resembles and serves as a flat-top desk. When removed, the gaming section is exposed, showing a backgammon board in ebony and ivory and socket for supporting a silver-plated candlestick on each side. Each player has a small drawer on his right for the discs that are used in the game.

Another popular gametable was the *bouillotte,* which is circular and generally made of mahogany with an open-work brass gallery, brass trim and a marble top. It was

Louis XVI gilt
bronze *bouillotte*
lamp from Chantilly

equipped with two small drawers and two little slides fitted into the apron. Originally these tables had a *bouchon* or cork to fill the space between the marble and the top of the gallery. This was slipped in when a level table top was desired without the interference of a gallery. *Bouchons* were also covered in leather on one side and green baize on the other, but very few of them remain. They were probably used very little and therefore stored or broken, and eventually lost. Today *bouillotte* tables are very popular items of decoration in French rooms, but without their *bouchons* their original multiple use, so dear to the French heart in the latter part of the eighteenth century, is no longer possible, nor, apparently, desired. More often than not, a *bouillotte* table serves primarily to hold a lamp.

Louis XVI *tricoteuse*
by Riesener

All sorts of mechanical
devices were invented, such
as *tables à ouvrage,* work tables, *liseuses,* reading tables,
and the *semainier* of the Louis XV period developed into the
chiffonier, usually in mahogany of the Louis XVI period.

The drop-leaf desk known as a *secrétaire à abattant*
which was already known in the Louis XV period was
produced in far greater number
under Louis XVI. Under the
marble top there is a drawer,
below which is the drop-
leaf section and a cup-
board with two doors
under the writing
surface.

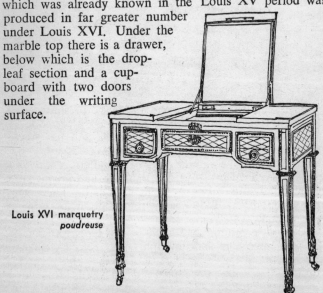

Louis XVI marquetry
poudreuse

Louis XVI commode
by C. Topino

The *bureau à cylindre,* roll-top desk, became popular during the Louis XVI period. Its base is very much like the typical *bureau plat* flat-top table desk of the Louis XV and Louis XVI periods with the addition of a superstructure fitted with many little drawers and a top which covers the whole writing surface as well as the drawers when closed, and which rolls back and disappears into the structure of the desk itself when opened. Some of these roll-tops are of solid wood, shaped in a curve; others are of slats, fastened together. Often there are three small drawers above the roll top, surmounted by a bronze galleried marble top.

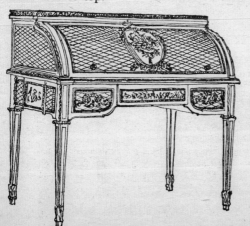

Louis XVI *bureau
à cylindre*
(roll front desk)
by Riesener

Louis XVI lacquer
secretaire by P. Garnier

Guéridons, round tables, were made in every size from the tiny candle-stand type with a ratchet system in the single support of the bronze-galleried marble top, to over-sized *bouillotte* tables and three-tier *servantes.* Again, most of these were made in mahogany and the famous *ébéniste* Weisweiler produced some still larger, round tables of very high quality with the interwoven stretchers between the legs which are characteristic of his models.

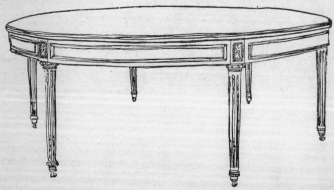

Louis XVI library table by Riesener for Versailles

The *rafraîchissoir* introduced in the Louis XV period, grew in popularity during the Louis XVI period and was made in considerable quantity. In the provinces, walnut and fruitwood were widely used as well as oak, and the wine bottle holders in them were made of tole or of iron.

Around 1772 *le medaillon* or oval back appeared on

Louis XVI gilded armchair
by Fromageau

chairs. As mentioned earlier, chair legs which at first had remained slightly curved, straightened out and the shell and flower motifs in the carving were replaced by pearls and ribbons. Some chairs had backs in the form of lyres, and lyres were also used for the bases of tables.

The arms of the straight-legged chairs of this period were again brought forward and rose directly above the front legs as they had before the Régence and Louis XV period. Although the base of the arms returned to their former position, the arms themselves often receded and curved between that starting point and their joining the back. The straight legs were usually fluted and terminated

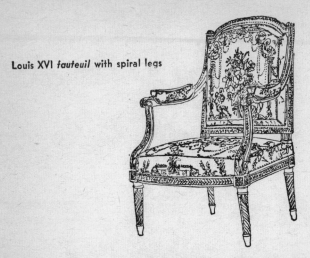

Louis XVI *fauteuil* **with spiral legs**

in small square blocks decorated with a carved rosette. A spiral leg, which is more unusual than the fluted leg, is generally a sign of quality and special designing. This is not to say that some of the finest chairs made by the great Georges Jacob did not have fluted legs, since most of them did. It merely means that spiral legs are generally con-

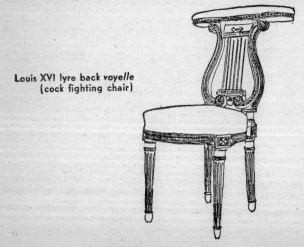

Louis XVI lyre back *voyelle*
(cock fighting chair)

Louis XVI *marquise*

sidered interesting and different and seem to be found only on chairs of excellent quality.

This treatment of legs in furniture brings me to a discussion of the first dining tables to be made in eighteenth-century France. They were first seen during the Louis XVI period and made by such *maître ébénistes* as Canabas and his followers. Of solid mahogany, they are almost round when the drop-leaves are in position. The center splits in half and reveals a mechanism with two extra legs to support additional leaves. When closed there is an iron hook and screw eye under the top to prevent it from opening when used without leaves. Its legs are cut in eight flat surfaces rather than turned, and they are finished with brass feet terminating in casters, for greater mobility.

As these tables are extremely scarce, the small French dealers have struck on a way of producing somewhat similar tables from nineteenth-century ones which came into the world with heavy bulbous legs. These heavy legs are shaved down and turned, but since the areas between the great bulges are very slender, the newly shaved legs cannot be any heavier than were those thinnest sections. Thus, not only are they altered and faked, but the proportions are wrong and as a result they look ridiculous. Of course, they are relatively inexpensive and for those who do not appreciate the difference, they fill a great need.

A serving table known as a *console-servante* with a marble top and shelves below was very much in vogue.

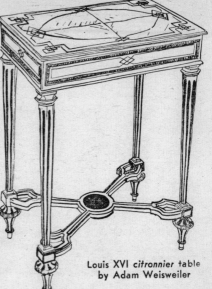

Louis XVI *citronnier* table by Adam Weisweiler

and another type with a drawer in the apron, under the galleried marble top and a wooden undershelf, known as a *desserte* was equally popular. With the advent of a dining table, other *console-dessertes* or *commode-dessertes* were created to accompany it and offer greater comfort and convenience for dining.

Louis XVI table made for Marie Antoinette for St. Cloud

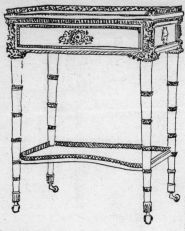

Louis XVI table
made for Gouthière
in 1781

Precious woods, straighter forms, and marquetry with the attributes of country life were some of the characteristics of the new Louis XVI style. Handles were fashioned in the form of rings with beaded edges, and rams' heads and hoofs were much in evidence. Mahogany, which had already been used during the Louis XV period, especially in such seaport towns as Bordeaux and Nantes which had access to it when it first arrived from the Indies, became a favorite wood in Paris and was most meticulously worked and enriched with very handsome and, frequently exquisitely chiseled bronzes.

Louis XVI
mahogany
servante

Louis XVI mahogany *desserte*, with marble top

In the late Louis XVI period the use of plain surfaces of wood, usually mahogany of a very fine quality known as *acajou mouchté,* which shows markings of waves and darker spots in the grain, gave furniture a new appearance, especially when mounted with the newly conceived bronze *plaque striée* (striped plaque), which was used on aprons of tables and commodes, and on their legs. At the corners of some pieces there appeared caryatides and women's busts which emerged from long sheaths supported by bare

Louis XVI *demi-lune* commode, with side cabinets

Louis XVI finely chiseled gilded bronze *gueridon* (round table) with malachite top

feet. Usually associated with the Empire period this treatment of Egyptian inspiration was already used by such cabinetmakers as Beneman, Weisweiler and Molitor at the end of the Louis XVI reign. Sphinxes also appeared at this time, inspired by the art of Greece rather than that of Egypt. Egyptian sphinxes are masculine, without wings, while Greek sphinxes are feminine and have eagle's wings.

Louis XVI lacquer table made for Marie Antoinette by Adam Weisweiler

It is clearly the latter type which was adapted in France from the Louis XVI period on.

The famous caryatides of the Erectheum in Athens inspired the draped women's figures supporting tall baskets on their heads, which became one of the most characteristic forms at the end of the eighteenth century. The palmette design also appeared at this time, and small flowers in bronze at the ends of legs which were now square.

Louis XVI *liseuse* with insets of Sevres plaques

Inset porcelain plaques, already used as early as the Louis XV period became more popular as cabinetmakers devised ways to show them to greater advantage. Another innovation was furniture entirely of metal, some in gilded bronze, in green bronze, in wrought iron and some even in steel, usually with marble tops. These were used most successfully for round tables and other odd pieces, sometimes combining the use of metal with porcelain plaques or Japanese lacquer. Chairs and beds were painted Trianon gray or white, sometimes with touches of green or blue, and sometimes they were gilded. Paneling was also painted, often relieved with touches of gold or color.

It was the day of the boudoir or intimate room and color prints decorated the walls, depicting the more relaxed life of the period. People enjoyed pictures which told a story or showed an interior containing elegant figures. Painters such as Greuze, Hubert Robert, Mmes. Vigée Le Brun and Vallayer Coster were very popular. Color prints by Janinet, Debucourt and Lavreince, for example, and Mallet's gouaches, give one a good idea of the interiors of the period.

Louis XVI paneling from Avignon

Window draperies were full and made of luxurious satins, *lampas,* and *dauphines.* Alcoves were built for beds and *canapés* and for *lits de repos* or day-beds. Canopies with sculptured doves, arrows and similar symbols of love and tenderness were very much in vogue, and pearls and ribbon designs abounded in all materials, whether marble, wood, bronze, porcelain or silks.

A new form of upholstery was devised called *en tableau*. A sharp ridge accentuating the straight lines was outlined in gimp or elaborate passementerie, and gave a very elegant and sumptuous look. This type of upholstery requires great skill and relatively few upholsterers in the world are able to handle it successfully, but it adds great style when well done.

One of the great cabinetmakers who started his career during the reign of Louis XV but went on into the Transition period was Roger Vendercruse LaCroix. Another was Claude Charles Saunier who began to work in the Louis XV style and suddenly plunged into the Louis XVI style for the rest of his life. Typically Louis XVI in character was the work of the great Jean Henri Riesener, Jean François Leleu, Martin Carlin, Adam Weisweiler, and Beneman among others. A separate chapter which is devoted to some of the outstanding furniture makers of the eighteenth century will supply additional information to those who are interested.

It is a surprising and a curious fact that a great percentage of the furniture made during the reigns of Louis XV and Louis XVI is still intact, either in museums or in private collections, while that of the Louis XIV period has all but disappeared. After the French Revolution, the English bought conspicuously at the great sale of furnishings of the Palais de Versailles. Whole shiploads of furniture and works of art were transported across the Channel and thus were happily conserved for posterity.

Late Louis XVI *secretaire* by Paffrat

CHAPTER FIVE

The Napoleonic Era and Bourbon Restoration

DIRECTOIRE

Historically the brief Directoire period lasted only the four years between 1795 and 1799, but the Directoire style came into being with the Revolution and can be said to have begun as early as 1792. It is actually the transition between the Greek style of the late Louis XVI period and the Egyptian style of the Empire. Directoire followed the basic Louis XVI shapes and designs with minor changes and added such decorative elements as griffins, sphinxes, tripods, palmettes, fasces, cockades and other

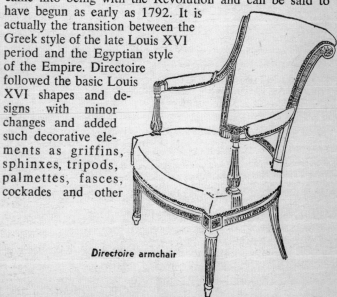

Directoire armchair

emblems of the Revolution. The classical influence of the painter David is apparent in all the work of this period.

Mahogany supplanted marquetry for solid pieces, or "case furniture," while those pieces which were painted often had touches of gilding. Arms again rose straight upward from the legs of chairs and *canapés,* while the legs

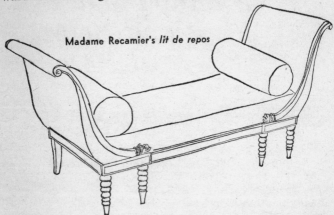

Madame Recamier's *lit de repos*

themselves were turned and smooth, tapering toward the feet where they often terminated in lions' claws and similar devices. Square blocks where legs joined the base of a chair were carved with flat rosettes, and swans, sphinxes and griffins were frequently incorporated into the arms. Another change was that tops of chairs curled backward, some with carved openwork in the form of vases, lyres and Greek keys. Seen for the first time, was a sofa called a *méridienne,* on which one was able to recline only halfway.

Horsehair was widely used and striped silk upholstery became very fashionable in this period. The often multicolored stripes were narrower than in the Louis XVI period, more closely spaced and no longer interspersed with flowers. Pastel shades were replaced by bottle green, bright yellow, mulberry and *aubergine* or eggplant. *Papiers peints* or wallpaper came into widespread use, with designs after Huet and similar to those of textiles.

In the decorative arts, the *bronzier* Gouthière often surpassed the high standards of earlier artisans in this field. The Greek motif gained further popularity as the *jardinières* and *brûle parfums* (incense burners) then in vogue, copied the shapes and models of ancient Athens.

CONSULATE

During the brief Consulate Period (1799–1804) Egyptian forms were developed which were the forerunners of the Empire style. Mahogany was still the chief wood employed, but lemonwood also became

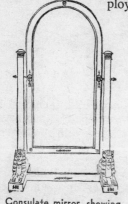

very popular. Its light color was a novelty and contrasted most effectively with the dark woods in which the new designs were inlaid. The changes that crept in after the Directoire were very slight indeed but are nonetheless apparent in the forms and shapes of ornaments and of bronzes. For example, ring handles gave way to rectangular drawer pulls.

Consulate mirror, showing Egyptian influence

EMPIRE

When Napoleon Bonaparte ascended the throne of his newly created Empire in 1804, the style known as Empire was born. His craving to dazzle the world motivated the decoration of the day in which the greatest luxury and richness were the keynotes. Massive mahogany was embellished with elaborate gilt bronzes with geometric lines and in order to glorify and remind the public of his Egyptian exploits, sphinxes, winged lions and other Egyptian subjects were incorporated into the impressive decorations.

The solid mahogany, pedestal-base round table was a conspicuous new feature of the time and the massive mahogany bed in the form of a sleigh was also typical.

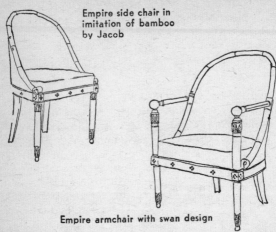

Empire side chair in
imitation of bamboo
by Jacob

Empire armchair with swan design

Many other new forms of furniture appeared, including a
shield-shaped dressing table mirror equipped with bronze
candle-holders and supported by a stand with a drawer;
a tall, standing pier-mirror known as a *Grand Miroir à
la Psyché,* also with bronze candle-holders; wash basins
in the so-called Athenian style; and dressing tables with
hexagonal mirrors and lyre legs. Mahogany bookcases
with glass doors in the upper half, large round tables with
their three legs representing winged sphinxes or griffons
and the weird combination of a winged Egyptian human
bust terminating in a
lion's leg, were other innovations.

The use of caryatides
which had been intro-
duced into the decora-
tion of furniture at the
end of the eighteenth

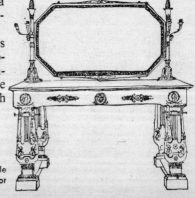

Empire dressing table
with mirror

century, became a formula in the Empire period. Caryatides rise from each side of a commode, a table, or even an armchair, bearing the weight of the marble tops on their heads and wearing Egyptian head cloths the two ends of which hang to their shoulders and frame their faces.

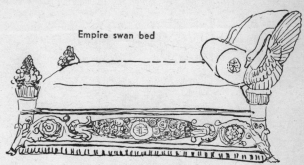

Empire swan bed

Many new motifs came into use, including the wreath of oak leaves tied with floating ribbons and garlands of vine leaves, pine cones, myrtle, clover and poppies as secondary decorative accessories. More frequent and important were palm leaves, amphorae, tripods and horns of plenty, as well as mythological monsters, sirens and marine horses.

Animal forms were borrowed from eagles, swans, bees, butterflies and lion snouts. The human figure appeared as "Victory," bearing palms or blowing a trumpet and also

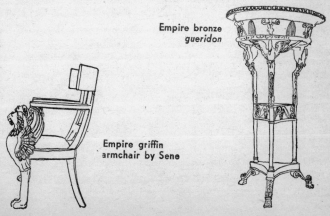

Empire bronze
gueridon

Empire griffin
armchair by Sene

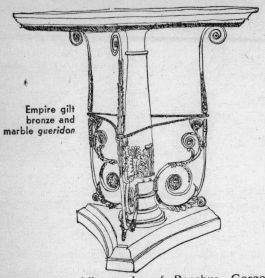

Empire gilt
bronze and
marble *gueridon*

as a dancer, while masks of Bacchus, Gorgon heads
wreathed in serpents, heads of Hermes, winged torches and
stars were much in evidence. All these were effectively
mounted in relief on mahogany furniture. The bases of
gilded *tabourets*, stools, were designed to resemble crossed
swords. Carved wood or gilt bronze fasces and draperies
decorated solid furniture, chairs and walls alike. Attributes
of war and antiquity were ever present reminders of the
new emperor's military might.

The architects **Charles Percier** and **Pierre François Léonard
Fontaine** were the most famous designers of the period
and many of their projects were carried out by their pupils,
Georges and **François Honoré Jacob,** sons of the great
menuisier **Georges Jacob.**

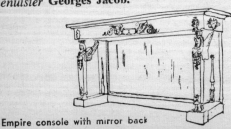

Empire console with mirror back

Upon the early death of the older brother, François Honoré worked with enormous success under the name of **Jacob-Desmalter** & Cie, throughout the Empire period. But the end of the Napoleonic reign brought on a crisis in the entire national economy and Jacob-Desmalter retired from active business and devoted the rest of his life to architecture and drawing. Later, however, his son Alphonse Jacob Desmalter continued the long family tradition by working for the Crown during the second part of the Restoration.

A great *bronzier* and gilder, Pierre-Philippe Thomire, was the artist responsible for the finest gilt-bronzes of the Empire period. Exquisite execution and a great majesty of conception marked his work, which still impresses the fastidious art connoisseur of today. Clocks intended for the Emperor's use were ordered directly from Thomire and Ravrio, who frequently signed their cases before they

Empire three drawer commode

were fitted with clock movements. The subjects of these usually large and elaborate clocks, were mythological. Whereas white statuary marble had been the favorite during the Louis XVI and Directoire periods, the taste changed to colored marble under the First Empire. Heavy satins in gold and green, or gold and red, decorated with bees and stars were favorite fabrics for hangings and upholstery. Heavy Aubusson carpets with green backgrounds covered the floors.

The great luxury and ostentation which had prevailed

under the monarchy was temporarily abandoned as the bourgeoisie gained supremacy after the Revolution. However the abolition of professional guilds had an even more disastrous effect on fine cabinetmaking than the disappearance of the clients who had encouraged and supported the profession. Relieved of all controls and catering to a

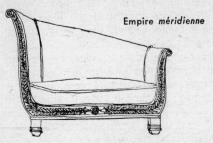

Empire *méridienne*

society without culture, many cabinetmakers produced poorly and hastily-made pieces completely lacking in artistic merit. In 1810, when Napoleon banned the use of mahogany for Imperial furniture and its importation, cabinetmakers turned to the local oak, beech, olive and boxwood and Ceylonese lemonwood. In addition to the poorer wood, cabinetmakers depended on strong glue to hold their furniture together instead of the time-honored system of doweling. With the exception of a very few self-respecting craftsmen such as the Jacob brothers, and the cabinetmakers Heckel and Pabst, the production of French furniture dropped to a very low level.

RESTORATION AND CHARLES X

Louis XVII was born in Versailles on March 27, 1785 and became the *dauphin* in 1789. He was imprisoned in 1792 and proclaimed King by the *emigrés* after the execution of his father, Louis XVI in 1793. However, this poor lad never left his prison alive, as he died in the Temple two years after he had become the titular King of France. The younger brother of Louis XVI assumed the title of King upon the death of the unfortunate Louis XVII, but he remained in exile, and not until the fall of Napoleon in 1814 did he ascend the throne as Louis XVIII. This period, during which the Bourbons were restored to their hereditary estates is known as the *Restauration* or Restoration.

Meanwhile the styles in furniture and decoration had undergone some changes. Mahogany, so much in vogue during the previous periods became scarce in France, and woods of lighter color came into fashion. Pear, cherry, maple, lemonwood and others were now found to be the best contrast to the dark brown inlay inspired by Dutch furniture.

Chairs acquired fan-shaped backs, alabaster was used for vases and opaline glass in soft colors, especially in lavender and blue, became the fashion. Horsehair and satin were still in vogue for upholstery and there were modified lyre-ends for tables with turned and bulbous legs and cross stretchers. *Méridiennes* were made with asymmetrical backs and the back supports of chairs curved backward more markedly than before. Boat-shaped beds in light-colored wood with sharply contrasting marquetry had solid heavy bases. Stools carried the arms motif in their decoration, and the X stool with slightly curved seat was also characteristic of the time.

Materials used for hangings and upholstery were not unlike those of the Empire period, but the bees and stars were things of the past. Odd, sharp colors such as electric

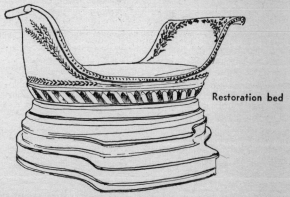

Restoration bed

blue came into use, while the more delicate opalines of earlier times grew strong and opaque, with shapes following the heavier lines of the furniture. Wallpaper designs simulated draperies, borders and festoons, with palmettes, braids and garlands of flowers in contrasting colors. Panoramic designs, called *tableaux tentures,* which used several shades of one color *en camaieu,* were also popular.

Charles X succeeded his older brother, Louis XVIII, to become King in 1824. The changes in style between the Restoration and Charles X are so slight and gradual that, except for some items of historical significance, it is almost impossible to pinpoint the dividing line. When Charles X was deposed in 1830, Louis Philippe was elected by the deputies and peers to succeed him, but by 1848 he too was deposed and fled to England, where he died in 1850.

While the lovers of French art of the eighteenth century regard the middle of the nineteenth as a period too depressingly tasteless to contemplate, we have, nevertheless, reaped a certain advantage from their passion for painting eighteenth-century chairs black. With infinite patience this black paint has, in many cases, been successfully removed, disclosing the original gilding, lovely white, or polychrome paint of earlier times. The paint has acted as a protective film, which though extremely difficult to chip off without the use of acids or abrasives, has nonetheless saved some splendid finishes that would normally have been ruined over the years.

PART THREE

CHAPTER SIX

Paintings
and
Drawings

In France the art of painting originated in the Church and over the centuries gradually became secular and decorative. The stone walls of medieval châteaux were hung with tapestries for warmth and the lively scenes they depicted also satisfied the need for decoration, but in the sixteenth century François I ordered paintings for the new, wood-

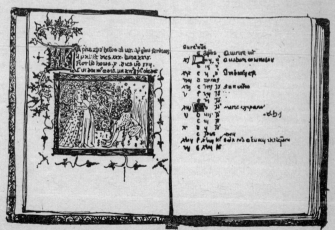

Page from a fourteenth century *Livre d'Heures* (Book of Hours)

paneled rooms of the châteaux at Fontainebleau, then being built by Italian artists, whose style developed into what is known as the "School of Fontainebleau."

During the reign of Louis XIV large paintings exalting the greatness and grandeur of the king and showing the courtiers in all their splendor, covered the walls of royal buildings. Landscapes with contemporary applications of mythological themes were carried up to and continued onto the ceilings. Small easel portraits and religious paintings also came into vogue.

In the Régence and Louis XV period the frames of wall panels were elaborately carved and decorated, leaving less space for pictures, which became correspondingly smaller. The art of painting came into its own in the eighteenth century and was exemplified in the work of artists such as Watteau, Boucher and Fragonard. The sophisticated elegance and refinement of taste, coupled with great sensuality, which typified the age were apparent in paintings as well as all other forms of French art. In the Louis XVI period there was somewhat greater restraint, and a return

"The Annunciation" from a fourteenth century Book of Hours. Spencer Collection, N.Y. Public Library.

to classic lines gave the appearance of greater simplicity, although luxury and finesse were not diminished.

The Revolution which abolished the elegance of the Court had a simplifying effect on painting. Classicism was the pervading approach and portraits placed greater emphasis on the individuality of the sitter than on his surroundings.

In the Gothic period French ecclesiastical art was on the very highest level. Altar pieces, such as the great *Pietà* painted in Avignon, around 1460 and now in the Musée du Louvre, are masterpieces of spiritual, as well as artistic quality. *Livres d'Heures* or Books of Hours, reached a pinnacle of perfection at this same time. These richly illuminated fifteenth century prayer books with miniature paintings on parchment depicting scenes from the Life of the Virgin, the Crucifixion and allied subjects, are jewels of the art of painting.

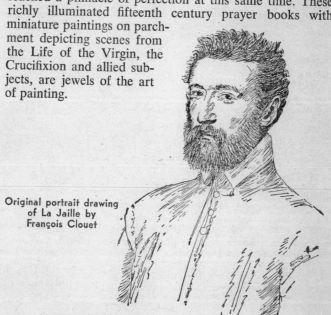

Original portrait drawing
of La Jaille by
François Clouet

Jean Fouquet who was born around 1416 and died about 1480, was attached to the service of Charles VII and Louis XI in the middle of the fifteenth century. His influence on the art which followed was very marked although little surviving work is indisputably by his hand.

His departure from purely ecclesiastical art to portraiture and historical scenes awakened a new conception of painting and an interest in secular subjects.

In the sixteenth century **François Clouet** (1522–72) and **Corneille de Lyon** (approximately 1530–60) were portrait painters of rare ability and their superb little oils, as well as pencil portraits heightened in sanguine (red chalk) are of the most exquisite finesse, and were undoubtedly extraordinary likenesses. Their sensitive portrayal of character caused their subjects to come alive.

Giambattista Rosso (1496–1541), an Italian architect and painter, who was called to Fontainebleau by François I in 1531, undertook the building of the Great Gallery. **Francesco Primaticcio** of Bologna (1504–1570) was commissioned by the King to fetch antique sculpture from Italy or to have copies made there for the decoration of the château. These two men greatly influenced the trend of French painting and architecture during the sixteenth century. When Rosso died in 1541, Primaticcio became the sole master of the work at Fontainebleau, where he was able to complete his greatest achievement; the decoration of the "Gallery of Ulysses" and the ballroom of Henri II.

During the first half of the seventeenth century such painters of note as **Georges De La Tour** (1593–1662) and **Eustache Le Sueur** (1617–55) were influenced by the Flemish School of painting. Of interest too, are the little-known **A. Baugin** (circa 1630) and **Jacques Linard** (1600–50), both of whom painted still life and flowers in a strong and delightful manner, reminiscent of the work of early Dutch flower painters, but essentially French in character.

In the graphic arts the uniquely gifted and highly original **Jacques Callot** (1592–1635) produced etchings of landscapes and had a genius for caricature and the grotesque. His series of etchings depicting the atrocities of the Thirty Years War, *Les Misères de la Guerre,* later inspired the English Hogarth and Goya in Spain.

Very different from the work of his contemporary, Callot, are the strong, somber paintings of **Louis LeNain** (1593–1648), which depict the peasants of his time in their daily surroundings and convey a sense of resignation to the deep tragedy of their lives. LeNain's paintings have a haunting, human quality which fills one with an emotional awareness of the lives and moods of the common people of his period. **Mathieu LeNain** (1607–77) also painted homely scenes of daily life with a great sense of architectural composition and with the formality which is typical of his time.

In the seventeenth century **Nicolas Poussin** (1594–1665), with biblical and mythological subjects in vast landscapes, emerges as a giant of his period. Poussin was appointed Court Painter to Louis XIII at the instigation of Cardinal Richelieu. He returned to Rome after the latter's death in 1642 and spent the rest of his life in Italy painting scenes of antiquity, with which he was so imbued that he strove to evoke the mood in his own works. His broad and noble landscapes, which were enhanced by classic architecture, were carefully planned according to the nature of his subjects and as a result of profound scholarship and reflection. A mystic quality guided him in the production of a timeless art. His paintings ranged from pagan scenes with nymphs and satyrs to a Crucifixion.

Claude Gellée known as **Claude Lorrain** (1600–82), painted biblical and allegorical figures in romantic landscapes, with a unique mastery of the moods created by effects of light and air. Claude's inimitable landscapes are not exact copies of nature, for he soars above precise representation into the realms of poetry and enchantment, and was the master of magic sunsets, sunrises and the sheer beauty of misty atmosphere. As a very young man he left home and went to Italy where he was employed in the household of a marine painter, Agostino Tassi. It is said that he worked there as a pastry cook and his duties included preparation of the artist's colors. After timid, inept attempts to copy Tassi's paintings Claude finally acquired the ability which enabled him to become independent.

It must be pointed out, that both Nicolas Poussin and Claude Lorrain spent most of their lives in Italy and that Claude and the incomparable Callot were both natives of Lorraine, not, at that period, under the jurisdiction of the King of France. Thus none was typically French and they had relatively little influence on French art of their time. It was over a half-century later that their influence made itself felt and they were generally accepted as belonging to the French school.

Under Henri IV the admirable tradition of pencil and sanguine portraits started by Clouet was carried on by **Quesnet, Benjamin Foullon** and the Dumonstier family of which two generations succeeded each other at Court. The most able, **Daniel Dumonstier,** was born in 1574 and died in 1646. These artists lacked the taste and linear precision of their predecessors, but nonetheless gave their work a very lifelike character. Very honest in their observation, they were never in the least flattering to their sitters.

The Flemish artist **Pourbus the Younger** who worked in France from 1606 until his death in 1632 modified this style of portraiture and painted formal, official likenesses of standing subjects. Heavy draperies, architectural backgrounds with furniture and other objects, augment the effect of majesty and elegance in his paintings. **Philippe de Champaigne** (1602–74), whose official portraits were the most important part of his life-work, continued the formula of a standing subject with an elaborate background, but through his keen observation of faces and remarkable technique, his paintings are far superior to those of Pourbus. His portrait of Cardinal Richelieu and that of "Louis XIII Crowned by Victory" are splendid examples of his art.

Robert Nanteuil (1623/30–1678) became known for his very fine pencil portraits and was appointed designer and engraver to the royal cabinet by Louis XIV. In 1660 due to Nanteuil's influence, the King proclaimed the art of engraving free and distinct from the mechanical arts, and engravers became entitled to the privileges of other artists. Such revolutionary strides were being made in the art of engraving at this time, that Nanteuil was able to express his unique talent and attain perfection in his portrait engravings.

Charles LeBrun (1619–90) had studied under Poussin and in 1661 as his first royal commission, he painted a series of subjects from the life of Alexander. Louis XIV, who considered himself a second Alexander, was greatly flattered and LeBrun subsequently became Court Painter and head of the French Academy. His paintings demonstrated talent but had little emotional quality and LeBrun's greatest ability lay in the field of decoration.

Nicolas (1606–68) and **Pierre Mignard** (1612–95) were also portrait painters. Pierre, who was very popular at Court, opposed the authority of LeBrun and was therefore denied large public commissions. In consequence he concentrated on portraiture and painted all the beauties and important people of his day. Thanks to his longevity, Pierre Mignard enjoyed the great satisfaction of succeeding his enemy LeBrun as "First Painter to the King."

In the late seventeenth century the position of women improved and one sees more female portraits than before. **Hyacinthe Rigaud** (1659–1743) however is best known for his portraits of noblemen in full regalia. His portrait of Louis XV as a child combines the pomp and formality of his royal subject with the very appealing face of the boy. In his youth Rigaud was under the guidance of Charles LeBrun; in 1702 he was elected to the Academy and in 1733 became its Director.

Nicolas Largilliere (1656–1746), a historical painter and portraitist, was received at the Royal Academy in 1686 and finally became its Director and Chancellor in 1743. He was an expert in depicting femine beauty and composed collective portraits with great dexterity.

One of a series of decorative paintings on a panel representing the Zodiacal months of the year; this one depicts Leo and Virgo

François Hubert Drouais (1727–75) was a fashionable portraitist and miniaturist of the Louis XV period, who was favored by women because he showed them to such advantage. Madame de Pompadour sat for him in the latter years of her life. His painting of Madame du Barry as a vestal virgin in transparent draperies created a scandal at the Salon of 1771. He also painted a charming official portrait of the "Royal Children of France" against a pastoral background. Drouais' depiction of intimate family groups in their private rooms was a pleasing departure from the usual studied poses.

In the early eighteenth century pastel became a popular medium. **Maurice Quentin de La Tour** (1704–88) and **Jean Baptiste Perroneau** (1715–83) were two rival pastel portraitists of unusual ability and charm. Their expressive and lifelike portraits, especially in the case of La Tour and the enchantingly soft colors and elegance of Perroneau's work evoke our admiration.

The love of spectacles and the theatre was great in France as early as the seventeenth century, and troupes of traveling Italian actors enjoyed tremendous popularity

Flower print by
J. B. Monnoyer
(1636 - 1699)

at Court. Richelieu is known to have loved the theatre and Henri IV and Louis XIII enjoyed the farces of the Italian Comedy enormously. While the latter did not actually act, he did participate enthusiastically in the entertainments such as masquerades, ballets and other fêtes at Court. There was little or no scenery, and until 1634 when a piece by Corneille was performed at the Galerie du Palais, there were no female roles. In 1637 a permanent theatre was established in Paris and in 1643 Molière added another. In the Italian Comedy the characters, such as Harlequin, Scaramouche, Pierrot, and later, when women were included, Violette, were fixed, and each had his traditional, fantastic costume. When performances became more regular and comedies and tragedies were presented, this changed, but it was a very slow evolution and meanwhile Italian Comedy figures were synonymous with the theatre.

With such amusements in vogue, French painters of the late-seventeenth and early-eighteenth centuries painted stage scenes with harlequins and ladies. The influence of Jacques Callot, who had been dead for over fifty years, is apparent in the painting of **Claude Gillot** (1673–1721) one of the most noted painters of theatrical and grotesque scenes of his time. As he was the master of **Antoine Watteau** (1684–1721) the same theme appears again in Watteau's paintings, as well as in those of his many imitators. The object was to evoke memories of romance and mystery and to recapture delightful and illusive, enchanted moments.

Trade with the East India Company fired the imagination of all French artists and Watteau painted panels in the Chinese manner, depicted scenes in park settings, and romantic *fêtes galantes,* enjoyed by elegantly appareled ladies, serenaded by handsome cavaliers.

Watteau, whose parents were too poor to help him cultivate his genius, left Valenciennes in 1702 and attached himself to a scene painter with whom he travelled to Paris and whom he assisted in painting theatrical decorations. Later, abandoned by his companion, he was fortunate in meeting Claude Gillot who recognized his great talent and taught him all he knew. Watteau's style was the perfect expression of the spirit of the early eighteenth

"The Village," pen and ink, brush and wash drawing over red chalk, by
Honoré Fragonard (1732-1806)

century at its best, with all the grace and charm of that
delightful period. His wonderful sanguine and pencil drawings show him to have been a superb draftsman as well
and even the slightest of his sketches is an important
adjunct to any art collection.

Nicolas Lancret (1690–1743) and **Jean Baptiste Joseph
Pater** (1695–1736), imitated Watteau's style, incorpo-
rating into their scenes of an imaginary, glamorous world,
negro servants, Turks, Sultans, peasants, shepherdesses
and Indian subjects. "Singeries" in which monkeys filled
the roles of men were added by Desportes, Van Loo and
Boucher. **François Desportes** (1661–1740) a famous still
life painter, depicted silverware, rich materials and trophies
of the hunt complete with game. He also painted the dogs
of Louis XIV and Louis XV. **Charles Amedée Philippe Van
Loo** (1705–65), who came of a family of Dutch origin,
painted portraits of individuals and of groups in a charming if somewhat stilted manner. He was called to Prussia
by Frederick II where he assisted in the decoration of the
palace of "Sans Souci" in Potsdam.

François Boucher (1703–70), the most admired painter

of the latter half of the eighteenth century, was a pupil of François Le Moyne and in 1727 went to Rome with the painter Charles Van Loo. Attracting the attention of Madame de Pompadour he became "First Painter to the King" and later Director of the Academy and Designer of the Beauvais factory. His compositions were rich and voluptuous and his great technical skill and exquisite coloring are especially apparent in his painting of nudes. He painted women in their boudoirs, dressing or reclining, and Venus and cupids against pastoral backgrounds. The flesh tints painted with unprecedented charm produced a fairytale atmosphere. Further evidence of his ability as an artist are his pencil drawings in which the perfection of line is augmented by the perfect balance of his compositions.

Toward the end of the century mythological and Biblical scenes were treated in a light vein and used mainly as a vehicle for amorous themes. Then this expedient was abandoned in favor of a franker approach. Idealized Court scenes in rustic settings became the vogue and with them came an awakening to the beauties of nature. Portraits became less stiff and showed people in more natural positions. Some were reading, others writing, and some playing with pets.

Jean Marc Nattier (1685–1766) portrait painter to the Queen Marie Leczinska and the daughters of Louis XV, made flattering canvases of glamorous ladies with pink and white cheeks, usually cunningly accentuated by a blue gown trimmed with lace and ribbons.

One of the most remarkable painters of this period was **Jean-Baptiste-Siméon Chardin** (1699–1779) who painted still life and simple scenes of daily family life in modest surroundings with such consummate art that they touch the heart in a very moving manner and leave a deep emotional impression. In 1728 he was admitted to the Academy and became its Treasurer in 1755.

Jean Baptiste Greuze (1725–1805) painted family scenes with sentimental charm and an excellent sense of color. Many of his pictures tell a story and are very sweet and appealing. His heads of young girls are among the best and most pleasing of his works. **Hubert Robert** (1733–1808), who spent much of his life in Italy, is known chiefly for his idealized paintings of Roman ruins and parks which he did in a masterly fashion, lending charm and lightness to scenes which were generally handled in an academic manner. A portrait of an intellectual woman seated at her desk was a departure from his characteristic dreamlike landscapes with figures and illustrated the new concept of women in France. **Claude-Joseph Vernet** (1714–89), another painter who spent years in Italy, specialized in marine and port scenes and painted a series of "The Seaports of France" for Louis XVI.

Jean Honoré Fragonard (1732–1806) a pupil of Chardin and of Boucher, like Hubert Robert spent a good deal of time in Italy, where he developed a light touch and freshness of color which he utilized in his enchanting paintings for the decorations of panels of complete rooms. He was the master of the ethereal painting and in his fine drawings proved himself to be a magnificent draftsman.

Madame Vigée Le Brun's (1755–1842) portraits are unusually pretty and painted with great skill and grace. She left France at the beginning of the Revolution and enjoyed great success in all of the many countries in which she lived.

In the eighteenth century easel paintings supplanted the huge canvases of earlier periods and were fitted into the panels of *boiseries*. When paintings by the masters were beyond the reach of the householder, obscure but not untalented painters did murals and panels in Chinese lacquer, *vernis Martin* or gouache. By the end of the eighteenth century wallpapers, usually depicting scenes with people and animals, were on the open market. Later, there were floral designs as well and the great need for paintings as wall decorations diminished. During the nineteenth century pictures were painted more as an expression of an inner urge of the artist than for the purpose of covering a blank wall.

Jacques Louis David (1748–1825) who had been a pupil of Boucher and also spent the early years of his life in Rome, was the first to return to antiquity, and was a forerunner of classicism, although he retained realism and charm in his portraits. An active participant in the Revolution, he subsequently attracted the attention of Napoleon,

St. Mary Magdalen, Gothic - Renaissance transition limestone figure, School of Troyes, circa 1520

Limestone figure, 1150-1200, School of Chartres

who named him "First Painter to the Crown." David's huge formal paintings glorifying the Emperor and the Empire seem over-literary by our standards and are probably less appreciated today than his really extraordinary portraits. David's pupil, **Baron Jean-Antoine Gros** (1771–1833) became attached to Napoleon from the time of his campaign into Italy and was the historic painter of the Napoleonic period.

Another of David's pupils, **Jean Auguste Dominique Ingres** (1780–1867) demonstrated an amazing technique which included a purity and clarity of line combined with perfect control of his medium. His portraits and nudes are unique, his charcoals extraordinary and his pencil drawings, using the finest lead point, are masterpieces of perfection.

Pierre Paul Prud'hon (1758–1823) never abandoned the grace of the eighteenth century and was a draftsman of exceptional quality with masterly ability in the portrayal of nude figures. His style bridged the gap between the eighteenth century and the romanticism which followed.

Rebellious against the dogmatic rules of classicism laid down by David, **Théodore Géricault** (1791–1824) painted death and human misery in a highly dramatic fashion. The salon of 1812 exhibited his "Cavalry Officer on Horseback" and his reputation was established immediately. His "Raft of the Meduse" exhibited in the Salon in 1819 precipitated the struggle between the Classic and Romantic Schools.

Seven years Géricault's junior **Eugène Ferdinand Victor Delacroix** (1798–1863) opposed the academic theories of painting which had been followed in France for over two hundred years and led the attack against the classical trend. He was an innovator in his treatment of color and its relation to light and chose classical, historical and liter-

Bust of Louis de France, Grand Dauphin, by Charles Antoine Coysevox
(1640–1720)

ary subjects as vehicles for the expression of strong emotion. He is considered one of the first painters of the Romantic School.

From time to time fine paintings of the French masters become available through the dissolution of an estate; the finest are extremely valuable, whereas lesser works are sometimes within the reach of a private collector. Very fine drawings are difficult to come by, although some pleasant examples of the lesser masters are still available. Some collectors prefer them to paintings because their spontaneity brings one closer to the artist's creative spirit. Drawings have a special interest and charm for the knowledgeable and scholarly collector.

CHAPTER SEVEN

Sculpture

Sculpture in France began with the building, in the twelfth and thirteenth centuries, of the great cathedrals of Chartres, Sainte-Chapel and Notre Dame. During the Gothic period while the Court was established in the Loire region, the art of sculpture, which was closely connected with architecture, developed on very sober lines. The churches were decorated with limestone statues of saints and gargoyles, and on secular buildings there were statues of kings.

Charles VIII visited Naples in 1495 and was so enchanted by its climate and beauty that he brought Italian artists back to France with him. Among these were two sculptors and two workers in alabaster, who in the service of the King, worked on the construction of the Château d'Amboise, the first royal residence of the period, and started the movement which developed into the Renaissance. With the building of the château at Fontainebleau during the reign of François I the style of the "School of Fontainebleau" was created. The greatest sculptors working in France in this period were the Italian, **Francesco Primaticcio,** the native artists **Jean Goujon, Pierre Bontemps, Jean Cousin** and **Pierre Delorme the Elder.** Their original works compared favorably with Italian art of the time. **Philibert Delorme** and his brother Jean were impli-

cated in a dramatic murder case after the death of Henri
II, but about four years later (1564) Catherine de Medici
commissioned them to construct the Tuileries, which they
did with unique and vigorous imagination.

Jean Goujon and Pierre Bontemps were Huguenots and
fled to Italy in 1562, after the massacre of Wassy.
Delorme and Primaticcio died in 1570.

In 1560 **Germain Pilon** received his first royal commission and made a group, called "The Three Graces" in the
form of a *cassolette* reproducing a type made for François
I by Raphael. This piece is typical of the elegance of the
pure style of Fontainebleau without any of the dryness of
previous works. Pilon received many commissions for
royal busts, effigies for tombs, coins and medals and before
he died in 1590, developed a style far removed from that
of Fontainebleau. His keen observation and execution of
portraits showing the psychological character of his sitters
made him the first French sculptor to free himself from
the medieval traditions and Italian mannerisms.

During the Renaissance sculpture was the art of kings.
Henri IV built the Place des Vosges and joined the Louvre
to the Tuileries. In the Louis XIV period the king was
glorified as the hero of allegorical subjects and the decoration of royal châteaux and parks, public buildings, monu-
ments and tombs afforded sculptors frequent opportunities
for practicing their art.

During his long reign, Louis XIV employed many
sculptors in the decoration of the various royal châteaux
he was building. The Palais de Versailles was the most
important of these and the great halls abounded in sculpture. Portrait statues of the "Great Men of France" including princes, admirals, marshals and celebrated soldiers
decorated the *Salon de la Guerre*. Statues of Richelieu and
other famous men occupied the courtyard, along with a
bronze equestrian statue of Louis XIV. Large allegorical
groups filled each intersection of the garden paths, which
were planned by Le Nôtre so that the vista could be enjoyed from many angles. Throughout the reign of Louis
XIV work went on without interruption but never reached
completion. Nevertheless Versailles is the supreme expression of the grandeur of France during "Le Grand Siècle."

Charles Antoine Coysevox (1640–1720) who became

the official sculptor to the King in 1666, was the author of many great portrait busts and much of the decoration at Versailles, which he executed in a formal and restrained style. Later, around 1700, when the aging Louis XIV commissioned sculpture for his château at Marly, Coysevox's style changed toward greater freedom and vigor and showed the first signs of the rising tide of the Rococo.

The nephews and pupils of Coysevox, **Nicolas Coustou** (1658–1733) and his brother **Guillaume** (1677–1746) continued this freer style. Nicolas Coustou undertook a great deal of carving for the Crown and worked at the Trianon, Versailles, and Marly as well as Les Invalides and Notre Dame in Paris. Guillaume produced a masterpiece known as *Les Chevaux de Marly* for the château there; an equestrian statue of Louis XIV, and a splendid bust of Marie Leczinska, which is one of the best portraits of the queen.

With the death of Louis XIV in 1715, the feverish building which had kept so many sculptors employed was greatly curtailed. Louis XV did not share his grandfather's passion for impressive royal palaces, but preferred intimate châteaux and smaller rooms. In addition, great changes took place in sculpture as private patrons wanting portrait busts and small, decorative pieces for their *hôtels particuliers,* or private houses, entered the market. Portrait sculptors attempted to approach nature more closely and to produce real likenesses, instead of hiding the defects of their sitters. The new interest in nature led away from pomp and formality and had a softening influence on art in all its branches. Decorative sculpture became less solemn, and many *rocaille* and asymmetrical decorations eclipsed the old forms.

Sculpture d'edition which consisted of small groups or busts which could be readily reproduced first appeared at this time. For these the artists chose bronze, terra cotta and even plaster, instead of the traditional marble. Most of the great sculptors of the eighteenth century also made models for the Sèvres porcelain works and designed biscuit figures and groups.

Jean Baptiste Lemoyne (1704–78) who enjoyed the favor of Louis XV and was commissioned to work for the

Crown, was responsible for many of the official statues of the leading political and professional figures of the period. He exercised great skill in an effort to make his sitters look realistic and to catch a fleeting expression. This was often achieved by a slight smile on their faces. Some of his sitters were dressed in the clothes of the period, others in antique classical draperies, depending on their preference.

Marble portrait bust of Louise Bongniart, by Jean Antoine Houdon (1741-1828)

The capital works of **Jean Baptiste Pigalle** (1714–85) were a monument to Louis XV at Reims, his famous *Mercure,* Mercury, and allegorical figures on buildings and tombs. A full-sized white marble portrait showed Mme. de Pompadour as *L'Amitié,* Friendship. A most welcome and delightful departure from his usual work are small groups of nude children. These are so true to life and utterly charming that one marvels at this sculptor's versatility. He was not a specialist in busts, although he made about thirty in his whole career, among which were ones of Voltaire, Diderot and a self-portrait. Place Pigalle in Paris was named after this great artist.

In contrast to Pigalle's work, **Étienne-Maurice Falconet** (1716–81) idealized his subjects, with the result that his models resemble actors playing a role. Mme. de Pompadour, for instance, was portrayed as "Music." Between 1757 and 1766 Falconet directed the modeling room of the Sèvres factory, during which period he created about a hundred porcelain figures. These were sometimes taken from Boucher designs and sometimes his own inventions. The "Falconet Children" as they are called, are shown engaging in various occupations in the city and in the country. When Falconet left, Pigalle came to work at Sèvres and made the "Pigalle children" which enjoyed an equal success.

August Pajou (1730–1809) who was the favorite sculptor of Madame du Barry later became the official sculptor of King Louis XVI and was then commissioned to make busts of the "Great Men of France" of his period. These life-sized portraits were the exception to the popular small sculpture then in vogue. Pajou made at least a dozen portraits of Mme. du Barry and many busts of more humble subjects such as his parents, and friends.

Jean-Jacques Caffieri (1725–92) supplied the series of "Great Men of France" with a life-sized bust of Molière, and all of his work is marked by great liveliness and vigor, especially suited to some of his models who were actors and actresses of the Comédie Francaise.

With **Jean Antoine Houdon** (1741–1828) the art of portrait sculpture reached its pinnacle. His portraits of Voltaire, Diderot, Rousseau, and Bouffon as well as Benjamin Franklin and George Washington, are masterpieces which show the true character of the sitter with great sensitivity. His women's portraits and those of children are touchingly beautiful and seen through gentle, kindly eyes. Nonetheless they are imbued with the same strength, harmony and serenity which pervades all his work whether done in marble, terra cotta, bronze or in plaster.

The so-called drawing room sculpture on a small scale was admirably suited to the work of **Claude Michel Clodion**

(1738–1814) who was the master of modeling nymphs
and satyrs, bacchants, cupids and other figures of pagan
origin, inspired by antiquity. Clodion's style greatly influenced furniture design, especially that of torchères,
candelabra, vases and furniture mounts, often executed
by the great *bronzier* Gouthière. Clodion's art expressed
veiled sensuality in a very delicate form and is the most
typical expression of French taste at the end of the
eighteenth century.

The art of sculpture suffered a greater setback during
and after the Revolution than any other in France and
little of note was produced until after the middle of the
nineteenth century.

CHAPTER EIGHT

Tapestry

In Europe the art of tapestry weaving was practiced originally for the purpose of covering stone walls in a pleasing and interesting manner and for keeping out the cold. Tapestries were also used to cover furniture, screens and, beginning with the Louis XIV period, floors. However, tapestry weaving had been known to the ancient Egyptians over three thousand years ago. A fragment of polychrome weaving was found in the tomb of Thutmose IV (app. 1400 B. C.) and is now in the museum at Cairo. Tapestries were also woven in Tyre and Sidon and introduced into Greece by Alexander; Babylon and Nineva excelled in tapestry which was much admired by the Greeks and equally appreciated by the Romans. Phidias is known to have decorated the Parthenon with tapestry and references were made to weaving in both *The Iliad* and *The Odyssey*. The art flourished in Europe from the fourteenth century until the eighteenth, when it gradually declined as new methods of wall paneling were developed. However, tapestry weaving has never ceased to be practiced and even in the twentieth century, they are being produced after designs of contemporary artists.

Tapestries were woven on looms by one of two methods. The most widely used was that of *haute lice* (high warp) in which the warp is attached to a wooden frame with

Detail of wool tapestry, end of the fourteenth century; Nicolas Bataille

roller top and bottom fixed between two heavy uprights at either end and held taut at all times with screws. There was also a *basse lice* (low warp) system similar to that used in weaving other fabrics, in which the threads of the warp were moved by pedals. The warp of antique tapestries was of twisted wool with some linen threads to give a better grip.

Through the sixteenth century, tapestry weavers wandered from place to place and settled temporarily wherever they had a commission to furnish tapestries for the château of a great noble, or for churches and monasteries. French weavers did not become organized professionally

Wool tapestry fragment, second half of the fifteenth century; "A Noble Company"

until the beginning of the fourteenth century, when they were known as *haute liciers,* or workers in high warp. During the Gothic period the Franco-Flemish tapestries and those made within the French boundaries resembled each other so closely that they are considered to be of the same school. Likewise, those produced at Arras and Tournai, which was French at the time, were almost indistinguishable.

Tapestry designs were copied from drawings or paintings called "cartoons" and the industry was always dependent upon artists, who frequently served as directors of various factories. As early as 1350 designs featured fleur-de-lys and coats of arms; soon after 1360 birds and small animals began to appear and were soon followed by human figures, religious scenes and others of contemporary daily life. Usually the names of the characters depicted were woven into the design. These tapestries were typically medieval in character, with scenes superimposed on each other, figures and gestures stiff and the folds of the draperies sharply defined in the Gothic manner.

Silk was used in tapestry weaving at an early date to execute delicate details, for backgrounds of sky, to heighten the luminous touches in draperies, and for ornaments and flowers. It was also used for hair, but never for flesh or faces. Gilded silver thread called *fils de Chypre,* was prepared in Genoa, Italy. The silver was beaten with hammer blows to strengthen it sufficiently to be wound around the silk thread which it covered completely.

Early sixteenth century wool tapestry; a hunting scene

Nicolas Bataille, who died in 1400, is the first name to stand out as a weaver and dealer in tapestries. Although most of his remarkable undertakings were destroyed, his principal work known as the "Apocalypse of Angers" still exists in part.

During the late fifteenth century France produced some of the finest tapestries the world has ever known. These Gothic tapestries with dark blue or red backgrounds strewn with flowers and tiny animals realistically represented, are known as *mille fleurs.* Among the most famous examples of these fabulously beautiful wall hangings are the "Unicorn Series" at the Cloisters (the Riverside Drive Annex of the Metropolitan Museum of Art of New York) and the famous set on a red ground in the Musée de Cluny in Paris.

Outstanding among *verdure* tapestries, a name given because of the predominance of trees, bushes, flowering green plants and meadows, which in one form or another have been made through the centuries, is a variety produced around 1500, known as *fleur-de-choux.* With great green leaves and yellow flowering shoots, these remarkable tapestries have enormous appeal and beauty, and are strangely lacking in monotony despite their repetitious and almost over-all design. During the opening years of the sixteenth century other fine tapestries were made showing many figures and elaborate scenes interwoven with gold thread; still Gothic in style.

The influence of the Italian Renaissance began to make itself felt at this time however, and the attempt of tapestry weavers to copy the subtle paintings of the Italian masters occasioned a drastic change in the industry. In 1519 a set of tapestries known as the "Acts of the Apostles" made by a Brussels workshop after cartoons by Raphael, was exhibited in the Sistine Chapel in Rome. Raphael's paintings had a depth and complexity which had never before been reproduced in tapestry and the innovation was widely imitated, although seldom successfully. French tapestries were outmoded overnight and this, after a long series of political and economic disasters, which had included the pestilence of 1418 as well as the hardships of the English occupation, caused a decline from which the French tapestry industry did not recover for more than a century.

An attempt was made to follow the new vogue, however. "L'Histoire de Saint Saturnin" dated 1527 and made for the Cathedral of Angers, breaks with the old forms so radically that it is believed the set was woven after the cartoon of an Italian artist. But this attempt to modernize the style of French tapestry had no future as not even the Crown showed any sign of encouraging its efforts. On the contrary, François I ordered tapestries in the Low Countries in 1532, 1534 and again in 1538, and gave an order to a Brussels dealer for tapestries in the Italian manner, enriched with gold, silver and silk threads.

In the middle of the sixteenth century the King decided to have the wall panels of his new gallery in Fontainebleau covered with tapestry and to that end set up a workshop on the premises. One tapestry is dated 1547, but François I died before the set was completed. During the reign of his son Henri II a group of four fine tapestries representing grotesque subjects, was woven at Fontainebleau. These are especially interesting because of their elaborate borders and the incorporation of the monograms of Henri II and Diane de Poitiers.

Under the patronage of Henri II a school for orphans was established in 1551, at which the pupils were taught the art of tapestry weaving in an attempt to resuscitate the art. Unfortunately, soon after the first students had matriculated and the school began to be fruitful, civil war broke out and ruined whatever remained of the tapestry industry in France.

In the seventeenth century Louis XIV's great Minister of Finance, Colbert, whose political ambitions for France included financial and artistic supremacy over her neighbors, reorganized and revitalized a number of her industries. Not the least of these were the tapestry factories which had languished during previous reigns. As Colbert's aim was to compete with the Flemish factories, he lured a number of able and experienced workers from their native land by offering them attractive privileges and installing them in the faubourg Saint-Marcel, the location of the Gobelins' dye works, as well as in the Great Gallery of the Louvre. These were joined by workmen trained in the earlier factories established by Henri II and Louis XIII. Under Colbert's new directives the Gobelin workshop was firmly organized on a very high plane in 1662. However, as it worked exclusively for the Crown it could obviously not satisfy all the minister's economic ambitions. He therefore encouraged the establishment of **Beauvais** in 1664. The latter also produced for the Crown, but accepted orders from other sources as well.

The court painter Charles LeBrun was named director of the **Gobelin** factory in 1662 and remained in that post for five years. During that period he was responsible not only for subject matter and composition, but also for the execution of the tapestries. Insisting on perfection, he submitted meticulously finished paintings to be reproduced on the looms and demanded the greatest accuracy, rather than simply supplying cartoons and allowing the artisans some freedom in the selection and disposition of colors, as had previously been done. During this period all subjects were chosen to exalt the majesty of the King, as a military hero, a great builder of royal palaces, or in some other flattering way.

After LeBrun left Gobelins to become Head of Build-

Early eighteenth century silk and wool tapestry made at Beauvais in the atelier of Philippe Bahgle after a design of Jean Berain

ings, and the tapestry industry was relieved of his severe ideas and discipline, the factory changed its entire approach. It began to work in *basse lice* and from paintings in a much lighter vein. Gobelins products reached the height of beauty in the grotesque tapestries on a yellow ground, designed by Jean-Baptiste Monnoyer after paintings by Bérain.

Because the State Treasury had been exhausted by the wars, Gobelins was obliged to close its doors from 1694 until 1699. After the factory reopened, it was for a time directed by the architect, Jules Hardouin-Mansart, who was followed by two relatives of the Marquise de Pompadour and then by several other architects until the painter

Jean-Baptiste Oudry took over in 1737. Oudry was followed by François Boucher from 1757 until 1770.

After its founding in 1664, the Beauvais factory was mismanaged and the replacement of Jacques Duplessis by Jean-Baptiste Oudry in 1726 snatched it from impending ruin. His cartoons gave the factory new life. Unlike Gobelins, Beauvais was a private enterprise, obliged to please and keep its clientele. Oudry understood the new demands, which were the result of an increased use of wall paneling. After rather timid beginnings, Beauvais, in the Louis XV period, began to make splendid tapestry furniture coverings as well as wall hangings.

Late eighteenth century silk and wool tapestry made at Beauvais under the direction of de Menou after a cartoon of Jean Baptiste Huer

Tapestries of the eighteenth century were treated as woven pictures and a carved and gilded frame was frequently woven as a border. In 1730 Oudry produced a set of tapestries called "Les Amusements Champêtres" and in 1732 a set showing scenes from Molière. After a number of similar designs he returned to more typical subjects and in 1736 made *verdures fines* (fine woodsy scenes). Not satisfied with the resources of his own imagination Oudry utilized cartoons by the best painters. He called upon Charles Natoire for cartoons relating the story of Don Quixote and on François Boucher, who within twenty years produced forty-five compositions—models for six entire sets of tapestries for Beauvais—all of which were of superb quality. Boucher succeeded Oudry as director of Beauvais, as well as of the Gobelin factory.

An outgrowth of the workshops which Henri IV had established in the galleries of the Louvre became known, during the reign of Louis XIV, as *La Savonnerie de Chaillot.* **Savonnerie** was the first French workshop to produce tapestry carpets and specialized in a unique rich, velvety type with knotted stitches for closer weave and strength. Furniture coverings and panels for screens were made in the same technique and designs were a profusion of garlands, foliage, floral motifs and birds, in strict symmetry, with the taste and style of LeBrun much in evidence. In 1712 Louis XIV granted Savonnerie the same privileges which had been accorded to the Gobelin factory.

The exact circumstances of the establishment of tapestry weaving in the **Aubusson** section are unknown, but in the seventeenth and eighteenth centuries privately-owned factories in the towns of Aubusson and Felletin strove to imitate the work done at Gobelins, Beauvais and Savonnerie. The king accorded Aubusson his protection in 1665, but the mark standing for the *Manufacture royalle D'Aubusson,* which was to have been woven in the selvage of each piece was frequently omitted. In 1789 Aubusson obtained authorization to make carpets in the manner of Savonnerie, but used no knots and made its carpets exactly as they made wall hangings. Beauvais supplied Aubusson with cartoons for many of their tapestries, but the Aubusson techniques were somewhat less refined and their weave coarser. After the Revolution the Aubusson factories functioned sporadically until 1819, when operations ceased altogether.

In the eighteenth century the demand for tapestry hangings declined as other methods of wall decoration were devised. Smaller tapestries were made to fit into the wood paneling and these in time were replaced by paintings and wallpaper. During the late nineteenth and early twentieth centuries there was a great vogue for antique tapestries. Those of the seventeenth and eighteenth centuries, particularly seat covers, were reproduced in great quantity. An experienced eye can easily detect the difference between

Sixteenth century Limoges enamel portrait of a man by Leonard Limosin (approximately 1505-1576). *Courtesy of The Frick Collection.*

Louis XIV carved and gilded console with Griotte marble top. *Property of the author.*

Louis XIV—Regence carved and gilded center table with legs in the form of "chimère" or fantastic animals. *Property of the author.*

Louis XIV carved and gilded mirror. *Property of the author.*

Louis XIV period André Charles Boulle *bureau plat* or flat-top desk. *Property of the author.*

One of a pair of Louis XV carved and gilded marquises. Signed: François Reuze. *Property of the author.*

Louis XV Coromandel lacquer commode with bronzes bearing the crowned C. Signed: M. Griaerd. *Property of the author.*

Louis XV bureau "en dos d'âne" or drop leaf desk. Signed: J. Dubois. *Property of the author.*

Chinese Celadon vase mounted in Louis XV gilded bronze by Duplessis.

J. Dubois desk—open.

One of a pair of Louis XV carved and gilded consoles. *Property of the author.*

Louis XV marquetry kidney-shaped table, open.

Pair Louis XVI carved and gilded fauteuils with a tag under seat of one with the inscription; "Chambre a coucher de la Princesse" indicating its place in the palace for which it was made. Signed: G. Jacob. *Property of the author.*

Transition marquetry oval table on three legs with colored woods. Signed: R.V.L.C. (Roger Vandercruse Lacroix). *Property of the author.*

Louis XVI carved and gilded small settee with back surmounted with a ducal crown. Signed: G. Jacob. *Property of the author.*

Louis XVI marquetry "table à Écrire" with various colored veneer, gilded bronze trim and gallery and rectangular legs. Signed: Joseph Schmitz.

Louis XVI three drawer citronnier commode with gilded bronze masking the drawer pulls on the upper small drawer. Edge of white marble top also banded in gilded bronze. By Leleu.

Louis XV-XVI transition gilt bronze table with tinted tortoise shell imitating lapis lazuli and green tinted ivory leaves.

Louis XVI ebony three drawer commode in the revived style of André Charles Boulle. By E. Levasseur.

Louis XVI delicately carved console, painted white with gilded details. Signed: J. B. Sene.

Oil painting on canvas "The Fortune Teller" by Georges de la Tour, 1593-1652. *Courtesy of The Metropolitan Museum of Art, Rogers Fund 1960.*

Portrait of Louis XV as a child by Hyacinthe Rigaud, 1659-1743. *Courtesy of The Metropolitan Museum of Art, Purchase 1960. Mary Wetmore Shively Bequest, in memory of her husband, Henry L. Shively.*

The Italian Comedy, oil painting on canvas by Claude Gillot, 1673-1722.

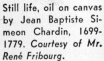
Still life, oil on canvas by Jean Baptiste Simeon Chardin, 1699-1779. Courtesy of Mr. René Fribourg.

"The Toilet of Venus," oil on canvas by François Boucher, 1703-1770. Courtesy of The Metropolitan Museum of Art, Bequest of William K. Vanderbilt 1920.

"The Bathing Pool" oil on canvas by Hubert Robert, 1733-1808. Courtesy of *The Metropolitan Museum of Art, Gift of J. Pierpont Morgan, 1917.*

"The Lovers Crowned," oil on canvas by Honoré Fragonard, 1732-1806. *Courtesy of The Frick Museum.*

One of a pair of sculptured groups in white marble of playing children by Jean Baptiste Pigalle (1714-1785).

"Grotesque," early eighteenth-century silk and wool tapestry made at Beauvais circa 1700 in the atelier of Philippe Bahgle after a design of Jean Berain. *Courtesy of The Metropolitan Museum of Art, Gift of Mrs. Guy Fairfax Cary, 1950.*

One of a pair of Louis XVI Gilt bronze mounted "Korean" porcelain saki bottles.

Pair Louis XVI andirons of dark bronze dog and cat mounted on gilt bronze. Model made for Marie Antoinette. *Courtesy of Mr. and Mrs. Benson Ford.*

Louis XV gold and enamel snuff box by Jean Moynat, Paris circa 1749. Courtesy of The Metropolitan Museum of Art, Bequest of Catherine D. Wentworth, 1948.

Louis XV period Verni Martin snuff box mounted in gold with the Paris hallmark of 1754. Probably by Alexis Gregoire.

Eighteenth century, early Louis XV period gold snuff box set with diamonds by Daniel Govaers, circa 1735. Courtesy of The Metropolitan Museum of Art, Bequest of Catherine D. Wentworth, 1948.

Mid-eighteenth century Marseilles potpourri vases from the Veuve Perrin factory, between 1750-1770. Courtesy of The Metropolitan Museum of Art, Gift of R. Thornton Wilson, 1950, in memory of Florence Ellsworth Wilson.

Eighteenth century Tournai soft paste portrait bust of Louis XV on gilt bronze base of the period. Circa 1760. Courtesy of Mr. R. Thornton Wilson.

Louis XV period Vincennes soft paste soup tureen and cover with green ground. Probably after a model by Duplessis. Circa 1753. *Courtesy of The Metropolitan Museum of Art, Gift of R. Thornton Wilson, 1950, in memory of Florence Ellsworth Wilson.*

Eighteenth century Mennecy soft paste small fountain and cover, with metal spigot, circa 1750. *Courtesy of The Metropolitan Museum of Art, Gift of R. Thornton Wilson, 1950, in memory of Florence Ellsworth Wilson.*

Pair eighteenth century Vincennes soft paste figures of a boy and girl modeled after Boucher by Bloudeau, 1752. *Courtesy of The Metropolitan Museum of Art, Gift of R. Thornton Wilson in memory of Florence Ellsworth Wilson, 1950.*

these and the originals however, for their weave appears tight and mechanical, while the original harsh colors of the reproductions are now faded to dreary tones of tan. They look lifeless, appear to have been painted, and are much thinner than those made in the earlier periods which they copied.

Seventeenth and eighteenth century Aubusson, Beauvais and Savonnerie carpets are in very great demand today, but almost impossible to find in practical dimensions, for those woven for the great châteaux were generally square and very large. After centuries of use, such tapestry carpets as are still obtainable are extremely delicate and need expert repair as well as great care. Wall tapestries are less in demand now because of a lack of space and the insufficient height allowed by modern architecture. Museums, however, are still keen buyers of an extraordinary piece, as are collectors who have the room to hang them.

CHAPTER NINE

Textiles

Painting and tapestries of the fifteenth century depict the heavy and sumptuous bouclé, velvets and brocades which France imported from Italy, Spain and the Orient for its use at that time. In 1450 Charles VII granted the city of Lyon a monopoly for the weaving of silk and François I in 1520 brought silkworms from Milan to be reared in the Rhône valley. At the end of the century Henri IV established a silk weaving factory in his own Palais de Tournelle, where they began making velvets, brocades and brocatelles. Progress was slow however, and not until the seventeenth century, with the energetic support of Louis XIV's Minister, Colbert, did the weaving of silk become an important industry. It then brought prosperity to the cities of Tours, Nîmes, Paris, and above all, to Lyon, which became the center of the industry.

Claude Dangon developed new methods and technical improvements at the Lyon factory during the reign of Louis XIV, and **Marcellin Charlier,** founder and director of the royal factory at Saint-Maur, was able to produce velvets, and gold and silver brocades which have never been equalled in magnificence. These were described in the contemporary inventory of "Furnishings of the Crown," but today have completely disappeared.

From the seventeenth century on, the quality and designs of French textiles reached such perfection that they surpassed those they had been imitating. The designers' fertility of imagination created marvelous new patterns with great branches, foliage, bouquets of flowers, architectural elements, ruins, columns, gardens with trellises, orange trees, and a wealth of other ideas. An extremely heavy and lustrous brocaded satin known as *lampas* became fashionable in France in the Louis XVI period and in the late eighteenth century printed cotton became popular and was produced in quantity.

During the reign of Louis XIV nothing was too rich for the decoration of royal palaces or for the clothing and houses of the affluent. Despite embargoes on the use of precious metals, the King made concessions to allow princes of the blood the use of gold and silver for richly embroidered clothing and furniture. Fabulous furniture coverings for the King's use were embroidered at a Gobelins workshop directed by Philbert Balland (active between 1670–87) and also by professional workmen at Saint-Cyr. At the convent of *Les Filles de Saint Joseph,* where Mme.

de Montespan had founded a school for impecunious girls of noble birth, much very fine embroidery was also done. Embroideries of almost barbarous splendor were made for *les Grands Appartements de Versailles* and remained in use long after the death of Louis XIV. The faces and flesh of human figures were made in chased, solid silver

Lyons silk *brochée* woven at Lyons in the second half of the eighteenth century, after a design of Philippe de la Salle plaques. Designs of trophies, columns, capitals, branches, gold flowers with colored silks and chenille, and at times even pearls and precious stones were embroidered in such profusion and high relief as to give the impression of sculpture. During the winter season these were used in the throne room of Versailles on *Les Meubles des Suites de la Paix*. This was the period in which the custom of changing upholstery fabrics and hangings for each of the four seasons was inaugurated.

It was also in the seventeenth century that France perfected the production of wool velvet or *moquette* also called *Velour d'Utrecht* because it was a specialty of that city in Holland. Much of it was woven in a single color with a stamped floral design, usually large in scale. The French also developed a type woven in many colors, depicting human beings, animals, châteaux, hunting scenes, draperies, tents and flowers on a much smaller scale. These materials were used as wall coverings instead of tapestries, and as upholstery fabrics in place of leather, damasks, and needlework which was usually in a large poppy design. Gilt-headed nails served as a finish where fabric was tacked to the chair.

Little by little the pomp and profusion were simplified and textile designs became less overwhelming. Smaller patterns on light grounds replaced the earlier elaborate types and floral motifs which closely resembled real flowers were skillfully entwined with branches and foliage. This change began to be felt around the year 1700 when **Jean Revel,** a pupil of LeBrun, began working at the Lyon factory. He achieved effects of light and shade, and made his subjects stand out in relief.

The greatest name in the production of silks in the Louis XV and Louis XVI periods is that of **Philippe de la Salle** (1723–1805), whose designs completely expressed the spirit of his time. Having studied in the school of design founded by François Boucher, Philippe de la Salle acquired the ability to express his ideas with the utmost charm. He combined chenille in his rich *brochés* and *dauphines* and his designs with animals, birds, flowers, ribbons, laces, palm trees, pagodas, landscapes and Chinese figures are compositions of unequaled lightness and beauty; never boring, always original and of unsur-

Eighteenth century flowered silk print of the Louis XV period

passed brilliance of color. Philippe de la Salle's fame extended beyond the borders of his native France and he was commissioned to design silks for the courts of Russia and Spain.

Jean Baptiste Pillement (1713–89) also deserves special mention for in addition to being a painter of note, he was one of the greatest decorative designers of his time. His beguiling textile compositions are justly famous. Other painters such as Lallié, Huet and Lajoue also designed silks, but as a rule the local Lyon designers were responsible for their own product. Although Lyon has remained the chief silk weaving center of France to the present day, there was always a certain amount of competition from other factories. Those of Soulas and Tour imitated Lyon silks and also made moiré silk, the secret of which had been learned in England, where this fabric originated. Silks woven in most of the factories in France were only nineteen inches wide, whereas those woven in Lyon were twenty-one-and-a-half inches wide. Hand-loomed silks are still made in the same width in Lyon today.

In the eighteenth century trade with the East brought many things to Europe, including printed Indian and Persian cottons, which enjoyed a great vogue in both England and France, where they inspired many reproductions. The designs of the first European cotton prints were produced from wood blocks, but in 1760 **Oberkampf** introduced a method of cylinder printing from copper plates, which greatly facilitated production. He established his famous factory near Versailles, in the valley of Jouy-en-Josas, where he found the chemical properties of the water to be especially favorable. Monochrome prints on a white or tan ground were made mostly in red, purple and brown. The toile of the eighteenth century with a blue design was of English origin. While Oberkampf used Boucher and Pillement designs for cotton prints, **Jean Baptiste Huet** (1745–1811) was the factory's chief draftsman and his designs included *"Les Plaisiers de la Campagne," "Le Marriage de Figaro," "L'escarpolet"* (the swing) and *"Travaux de la Manufacture"* showing how toile was made. Others depicted the fables of La Fontaine, "The Four Parts of the Globe" and popular events such as balloon ascensions.

Excellent toile was also made by **Dollfuss** and the **Koechlins** at Mulhouse. At the turn of the century factories employing hundreds of workers were established at Bourges, Montpellier and Nantes, where printed cottons imitated those from the East and whatever Lyon designs could be adopted. Charming and unpretentious *Toile de Jouy* was admirably suited to the decoration of country houses in the Louis XVI period and those which followed. It is still popular for informal rooms today.

A more formal fabric of the Louis XVI period was *lampas,* a heavy satin of wonderful quality woven with designs of classical inspiration. Red, yellow, green and, toward the end of the reign, light blue backgrounds were used, with scenes woven in ivory, with darker tones to give the effect of light and shade and to bring out the design as if it were in relief. The scenes, which were extremely varied, had architectural frameworks enclosing mythological figures, nymphs, satyrs, temples of love, cupids with their bows and arrows, love birds, flowers and all the motifs which were typical of the classic revival of the period.

Fine lampas of the Louis XVI period resembles a Clodion terra cotta group, transposed into luxurious and luminous silk. Used on furniture and for wall coverings and draperies it set off the straight lines of the period to perfection, and relieved them of severity and monotony. There are reproductions of Louis XVI lampas on the market today but designs have been altered and the repeats shortened to reduce costs, while the silk itself is too thin and flimsy to produce the right effect. One can still have lampas made to order, however, if one is prepared to pay a fabulous price and willing to wait two years or more for delivery.

The striped and flowered silks of the Louis XVI period are enchantingly light and brilliant in color. Often on a white or very light ground, small bouquets of flowers are strewn with carefully studied abandon in just the right position and number. Stripes frequently in sky blue, pink or other pastel shades are exactly the right width and distance from each other to give the most pleasing effect. Embroidered silk, done in *point de chainette* generally known in America as *point de Beauvais* was used on some of the finest palace furniture. Extremely delicate, it was only suitable for rooms which did not receive hard wear. Marie Antoinette had furniture covered in this lovely embroidery with her monogram worked into the design on the backs of the chairs. Hangings and bed canopies, too, were embroidered in this fashion on a white satin ground.

New velvets with very small, all-over geometric patterns were seen for the first time in the Louis XVI period and were used for furniture and decoration. A very special type which had tiny scenes and figures woven into the fabric, was developed for clothing, especially men's vests. This was the time of elaborately embroidered vests which were far lighter and daintier than those of the Louis XV period which had been heavy with gold and silver. Nosegays of bright flowers were not unusual on light satin grounds, often enhanced by spangles.

During the Directoire, silks were light in weight and similar to those of the Louis XVI period but more subdued in coloring; the stripes were narrower and used without flowers. The Empire period produced new designs with bees, stars and laurel wreaths as reminders of Napoleon's victories and might. Emerald green with a gold-colored pattern, and crimson with gold were the favorites, which harmonized best with the mahogany furniture ornamented in bronze.

One great textile genius emerged during Napoleon's reign to create pictures in velvet, a feat which had never been done before or accomplished since. In addition to portraits of Napoleon and prominent men of the period, **Gaspard Gregoire** (1751–1846) also made small pictures after Greuze, religious scenes after Raphael, flowers and still life. For many years it was believed that Gregoire's process was a secret. Actually, his method is known, but nobody has ever had the infinite patience and skill to duplicate it. By painting the threads of the warp he achieved an effect of transparency without any distortion of the original painting. Gregoire's velvets are very scarce and most of them are in the textile museums and a few private collections.

Joseph Marie Jacquard (1752–1834), the son of a Lyon textile manufacturer, invented the first wide loom, making a fifty-inch fabric and a technique for the mechanical weaving of very elaborate silks. His invention, completed in 1801, was not used until 1815, when it gave tremendous impetus to the textile industry by increasing production and reaching a much wider public.

During the reign of Louis XVIII eagles, bees and crowned "N's" were replaced by fleurs-de-lys and flowers, and the designs were heavier than during the Empire period. Under Charles X there was a movement toward the past and an attempt to reproduce the rocaille and floral motifs of the Louis XV period in a nineteenth-century style. These silks were of high quality but their most attractive attribute is a freshness of color and quaintness.

Some antique textiles are still obtainable, but seldom in large quantity, and they are growing increasingly scarce. Reproductions of antique designs generally tend to omit some details and can seldom equal the splendor of the originals. But today French silk manufacturers, especially at Lyon, are again making some beautiful silks based on their collections of ancient documents.

CHAPTER TEN

Clocks, Bronzes, Gold and Silver

In the tenth century mechanical clocks which functioned by a system of weights and counterweights replaced time-pieces powered by hydraulic means. In the fourteenth century there were a number of such mechanical clocks in existence in France. When in Nürnberg around the end of

Seventeenth century table clock

137

the fifteenth century Peter Henlein invented the main-spring, the whole approach to clockmaking was changed, and it became possible to make small timepieces. The first small, highly decorated cuivre doré (gilded copper) table clocks in the form of a hexagonal box with a horizontal dial originated in Germany in the sixteenth century. A few exquisite hexagonal watches were made in France around this time, but there were only seven clockmakers in Paris by 1550.

In the Louis XIII period, in an attempt to imitate German models, France produced some rather clumsy table clocks with heavy movements embedded in small blocks of ebony. Others were rectangular, with the per-pendicular dial in the front and a perforated dome which contained the striking movement.

In the seventeenth century the first wall clocks were made with tortoise shell cases inlaid with brass and finished at the top with a gilt bronze figure. These clocks were supported by a matching bracket, made for the purpose. During the reign of Louis XIV, André-Charles Boulle housed fine clock movements in highly decorated tall cases, known as *regulateurs*.

By the beginning of the eighteenth century, gilt bronze *cartels* (wall clocks) with and without the supporting bracket, made their appearance. Some were made in brilliantly tinted green or red horn, trimmed with gilt bronze. Others were lacquered with floral decoration in the *vernis Martin* style.

In 1753 Louis XV commissioned **Jacques Caffieri** to make an all-bronze case for an astronomic movement by Passement, which is still to be seen at Versailles. Other

Seventeenth century
table clock with
striking movement

tall clock cases were made in marquetry by the great French cabinetmakers of the eighteenth century.

Saint-Germain, one of the most famous workers in bronze during the Louis XV period, made mantel-clocks with an animal such as an elephant, a rhinoceros, a lion, or some other exotic beast in dark bronze against a background and base of brilliant gilded bronze. **Gallien** is also

Louis XVI watch set with gold, enamel and diamonds by Musson

Louis XV gold watch by Julien le Roy, 1772

known to have produced similar clocks. Other shapes and forms were developed to place on the mantel shelves, which were lower than in the Louis XIV period and required decoration. These were then flanked by candlesticks, candelabra, or vases of porcelain or marble, mounted in gilded bronze.

Watches in the Louis XV period were inclined to be round and thick, usually with double cases, and supplied with a gold key for winding. In the Louis XVI period they grew daintier and thinner, acquiring fancy shapes such as lyres, violins, and mandolins. They were usually enameled and often jeweled. Watches developed along similar lines throughout the nineteenth century, but deteriorated in taste and beauty.

Renaissance silver followed the general style of architecture and was elaborately decorated. In the Louis XIII period, candlesticks imitated square-based columns, and beakers were large, sometimes with spiral decorations. Throughout the Renaissance and Louis XIV period, ewers remained helmet-shaped.

Very little antique French silver has come down to us,

and what remains is highly prized by museums and collectors. Gold and silver were scarce, and successive laws banning their use caused existing pieces to be destroyed. The great goldsmiths of the seventeenth and eighteenth centuries were silversmiths as well, and some were also *bronziers*.

Lacking gold in the reign of Louis XIV, a throne of silver was made for Versailles. Many dressing tables and similarly fabulous silver furniture was known to have been made, but was melted down during the crisis of 1689.

Small silver pieces of this time were rather restrained in line, but often had rich chasing or engraving from designs in the de Cotte or Bérain style; with trellises, shells, scrolls, lambrequins and interlacing motifs; and frequently resting on a gadrooned foot. Tureens, wine coolers, sauce boats, candlesticks, covered dishes, plates and platters were among the more important household appointments made in silver, but cruet stands, mustard pots, beakers, egg cups, salt cellars and spice boxes also abounded.

Seventeenth century
Louis XIV Boulle
regulateur

One reads of the wonderful pieces made in the seventeenth century by the **Villiers** brothers; **Thomas Merlin** and **Pierre Germain,** who worked for the Louvre; and **Alexis Loir,** who published numerous designs for objects in gold, silver, and other metals; but alas, during the crisis of 1689

Louis XV bronze
mantle clock

most of these magnificent pieces ended in the melting pot and only their descriptions remain. **Dominico Cucci** (?–1705) an Italian cabinetmaker and sculptor who assumed French nationality, executed numerous pieces of furniture for the Court of Louis XIV and collaborated on ebony cabinets with bronze mounts, incrusted with stones and miniatures.

In China, when a precious porcelain had been broken, it was repaired with gold, without any attempt to disguise the repair. This Oriental idea spread to the West, and was first employed as an expedient to salvage some fine porcelains which had been broken. As this was so skillfully done that the piece was enhanced rather than the reverse, the practice of mounting soon included porcelains and marbles which were still intact. Some silver and a few gold mounts were made, but because of recurrent scarcities of these materials, French metal workers developed the art of mounting precious pieces in gilded bronze known as ormolu. The vogue took Europe by storm and every conceivable transformation was made. Oriental and European porcelains were mounted and transformed into ewers, potpourris and fantastic decorative ornaments; and *bronziers* made elaborate andirons, candelabra, sconces, vases, clock cases and furniture mounts.

Louis XV gilt bronze lantern

Bronze, which is an amalgam, or alloy, of tin, copper and zinc, is very malleable, yet extremely strong. It is also exceptionally close-grained, and consequently takes a very high finish when polished. As a rule, a sculptor would make a wooden model from which the *fondeur* would cast a bronze in one of the various methods then practiced.

One was a mold in clay or terra cotta, the other is known as *cire perdue,* or lost wax. The latter produced a finer finish, but as the wax was literally lost, it was necessary to have a wooden model from which to make future castings.

When the casting was completed, the rough bronze was refined and re-worked by the *ciseleur,* whose individual artistry was expressed at this stage. Next, the bronze was either cleaned in acid and lacquered, or gilded. In the eighteenth century mercury gilding produced wonderful results, but the process was so injurious to the health of the artisan that it is now against the law. In this method, mercury was mixed with pure powdered gold and spread on the bronze. It was then heated to a high temperature, which caused the ephemeral mercury fumes to rise, leaving behind a heavy coating of pure gold. The finished piece was known as ormolu, which is derived from the fact that the gold, *or,* was ground, *moulu,* to a powder to permit it to be thoroughly and smoothly mixed with the mercury. In the eighteenth century, the patina which bronzes acquire through exposure to air and dirt was not considered desirable and if such wear and dullness became apparent, the owners had the pieces re-lacquered or re-gilded. Bronzes were very rarely signed, but the famous *bronziers* had definite and recognizable characteristics which are of great assistance to an expert.

Louis XIV silver cup

Jacques Caffieri (1678–1755) was the outstanding bronzier of the Louis XV period and produced most skillful and faultless rocaille forms. He worked almost exclusively for the Crown and made a great variety of bronze objects including mounts for furniture. Most of his work is unsigned but we do know that he made the decorations for a mantelpiece for the Dauphin and also two chandeliers, now in the Wallace Collection. He signed a number of bronze busts as well.

Hallmarks on French silver usually indicate the name of the city or the locality in which a piece was made, and the control marks of a *Fermier Général* indicate the year of production. Some pieces also bear the maker's personal stamp which indicates his name, but unfortunately not all pieces have sufficient hallmarks to tell so complete a story.

In the Louis XV period as the prosperous business and professional class furnished their private houses, the use of silver became more widespread. Following the style in other fields, rocaille and asymmetrical shapes replaced those of the earlier periods, and decorations were molded in relief rather than being engraved. Silver of this period was melted down during the Seven Years' War, so it too is scarce. However, one superb work which is still intact is the nécessaire made by the Parisian silversmith **Henri Nicolas Cousinet** (1710–88), in vermeil for Queen Marie Leczinska on the occasion of the birth of the Dauphin in 1729. The set is composed of a tea pot, chocolate pot with spirit lamp, candlestick, spoons, sugar tongs, creamer, tea caddy, tea strainer, sugar bowl, snuffbox and a wooden chocolate mixer. The two chocolate cups are of white Chinese porcelain *(blanc de Chine);* while the sugar bowl and the tea pot are of Japanese porcelain with colored decoration, and two tea cups are Meissen imitations of the

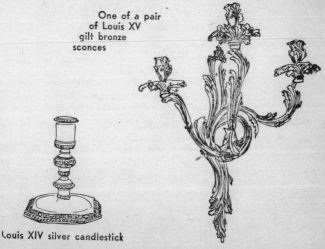

One of a pair
of Louis XV
gilt bronze
sconces

Louis XIV silver candlestick

Japanese. It is very likely that the latter were replacements made during the eighteenth century. This unique example of French craftsmanship was acquired a few years ago by the Musée du Louvre, where it is now on exhibition.

One of a pair of early eighteenth century gilt bronze and rock crystal *girandoles*

Another masterpiece by Cousinet for the Portuguese Court in 1757 is a table-ornament set of eight pairs of vermeil statuettes, representing the principal countries of the world in pairs of men and women in their national costumes. The countries considered at that time to be of greatest importance were England, France, Germany, Italy, Hungary, Poland, Spain and China. It is amusing to reflect that Portugal, which ordered the table decoration, was not represented!

In the Louis XV period coffee and chocolate pots were made for the first time and the first tea pot appeared in 1750. Wine tasters, ladles and all the types of flatware and cutlery we use today were devised at this time, including spoons and the four-tined fork.

Louis XVI large gilt bronze
barometer with steel
face, by Julien le Roy

Louis XVI *vermeil* (silver gilt)
coffee pot, circa 1770, by
Louis Joseph Lenhendrick

Claude Ballin II (1661–1754) nephew of a goldsmith
by the same name, supplied all the courts of Europe with
silver in the Louis XIV style even when rocaille forms
were already in vogue. On the other hand **François Thomas
Germain** (1726–91) reveled in the asymmetric forms
and launched the new rococo style. His designs for silver
and bronzes dominated the taste of the Louis XV period.
Juste-Aurèle Meissonnier (1693–1750) who like Germain
was a *bronzier* as well as a silversmith and ornamentalist,
showed the most fertile imagination in his designs. In
1726 he was given the title of *Dessinateur* (or designer)
de la Chambre du Roi. A pair of candelabra in the Musée
des Arts Décoratifs in Paris and a pair of candlesticks in
the Wallace Collection in London, attest to his extraordinary artistry.

Very beautiful gilt bronzes are attributed to **Jean-Joseph
Saint-Germain** a *fondeur-ciseleur* who was active during
the third quarter of the eighteenth century. His work was

Louis XV tureen and cover

of exquisite quality though considered a little heavy by some authorities. His stamp is found on three clocks in the Louvre, which represent only a part of his activity since he produced all forms of bronze objects. Three sculptors, known as the **Brothers Slodtz,** who were active in the Louis XV period are responsible for gilt bronze candlesticks, and mounts for porcelain and furniture which equalled in quality and beauty the best work of their contemporaries. Examples of their work are conserved in the Wallace Collection.

Nicolas Besnier (?–1754) **Orfèvre du Roi,** lodged in the Louvre, received many honorific titles and was ennobled. Early in his career he made a great deal of silver for Louis XV and later became a co-director of the painter Oudry in the management of the Beauvais tapestry factory.

Jean-Claude Chamberlano called **Duplessis** (?–1774) was a great sculptor and goldsmith attached to the Vincennes-Sèvres factory as a modeler. He designed porcelains and also made the bronze mounts for them. Appointed *Orfèvre du Roi* in 1758, he made the models for the mounts of the famous *Bureau du Roi* by Oeben and Riesener. Examples of his extraordinary work may be seen in the Wallace Collection in London, in Munich and the Petit

Trianon, where a large Chinese vase mounted in gilded bronze is on the mantelshelf in the dining room.

Jacques Roettier (1707–84) a son-in-law of the conservative Ballin, was also an outstanding goldsmith and worked in the Louis XV style from about 1750 until his retirement in 1772. His son, **Jacques Nicolas Roettier** worked for the Russian Court in the Louis XVI style from 1770 on. Other great eighteenth century goldsmiths deserving special mention are **Pierre Aymé** and **François Joubert** who made a pair of sauce boats for Madame de Pompadour which are now in the Musée des Arts Décoratifs. His style fluctuated between very rocaille pieces and others which were almost Empire. **Eloi Guerin, Jean-Nicolas Saget, J. T. Outrebon, C. P. Balzac, F. Vaucombert, Guillaume Loir, Filassier** and **Spire** all worked in silver with great distinction during the Louis XV period, some continuing into that of Louis XVI.

Robert-Joseph Auguste (1723–app. 1795), had acquired such a great reputation while working for Louis XV that

Early nineteenth century *vermeil* (silver gilt) coffee pot by Martin Guillaume Biennais (1764-1843)

One of a pair of eighteenth century silver candelabra by Jean Baptiste Ohéret

Mme. de Pompadour entrusted him to execute Falconet's design for her gold salt cellars. He later became official goldsmith to Louis XVI.

Louis XVI silver followed the fashionable classic influence of Delafosse and Gouthière and repeated motifs which were used in furniture, bronzes, and every other form of decoration. Publication of the notebooks on decoration by the architect and ornamentalist **Jean Charles Delafosse** (1734–89) exercised considerable influence on the development of the Louis XVI style. Delafosse's designs for gold, silver and bronze decorations combine rocaille motifs with those of antiquity. **Pierre Joseph Gouthière** (1740–?) was the greatest *bronzier* of the late eighteenth century. His style is easily recognized by his perfection of detail and superb workmanship. Gouthière specialized in decorations derived from vegetation, and other motifs included rams' heads, hoofs, and urns, sometimes topped with flames. A bronze mantel clock, *pendule d'Avignon*, presented by the town of Avignon to Le Marquis de Rochechouart, whose crest is at the top, is the only known work which bears his signature. Contemporaries copied Gouthière's style but never achieved his success.

Pierre Philippe Thomire (1751–1843) studied under Gouthière, who taught him the secret of matte gilding. Known primarily for his classical designs in the Empire period, Thomire made monumental table ornaments, candelabra and similar objects; the details of which were accented by brilliantly burnished highlights. He also made bronze furniture mounts for Jacob Desmalter. Vermeil was much in vogue in the Empire period and the elaborate table ornaments of **Martin Guillaume Biennais** (1764–1843) vied with Thomire's regal works in gilded bronze.

The classical forms decreed by Percier and Fontaine, the arbiters of fashion in architecture and furniture, were translated into silver and bronze during the Empire period as Napoleon Bonaparte sought to recreate the pomp and splendor of *le grand siècle* but the coldness of the prevailing forms militated against success. The abolition of all guilds left the industry without artistic control and the

Seventeenth century gilt
bronze small strong box with
engraved silver plaques and
very elaborate interior lock

production of fine silver was seriously hampered. During
the Restoration all rules were abandoned and silver and
bronze followed the tasteless innovations of the time; large
silver figures were decorated with enamel and stones and
parts of the silver were oxidized in order to accentuate
details. During the fifteen years between 1815 and 1830
silver became thick and heavy with compact groups of
flowers. Palmettes were replaced by acanthus leaves and
heavy gadrooning at the edges of plates and handles became characteristic of the period.

It is interesting to reflect how great a debt of gratitude
we owe to the various ambassadors to the Court of France
for their deep interest in her artistic achievements, during
the seventeenth and eighteenth centuries. Were it not for
their appreciation of France's silver, gold, textiles, bronzes,
furniture, and other artistic wares, many more of these
treasures would have been lost to posterity.

Seventeenth century Louis XIII
cut steel over green velvet small
box, lined in straw

CHAPTER ELEVEN

Snuffboxes and Other Bibelots

The nineteenth-century author, Henri Havard, writes that we must forgive our ancestors the habit of taking snuff since its main purpose was to kill the sensitivity of the olfactory nerves and thus spare its user the full impact of the many dreadful odors surrounding him. Not only must we forgive our ancestors, as we hope future generations will forgive the present cigarette habit (which has a less valid excuse), but we should be very grateful to them for leaving us the wonderful little boxes, the beauty and charm of which are well known to everyone interested in the decorative arts.

Louis XV perfume bottle

A gold nécessaire

In addition to snuffboxes, there were gold *nécessaires* or utility boxes, some of which contained writing materials, sewing equipment or manicure sets, and others perfume bottles with gold or silver tops. These, as well as lovely little patch boxes, called *boûtes à mouches,* which were similar to, but smaller than snuffboxes, bore inscriptions of endearment, usually in enamel on the gold mounts. Materials of every sort were employed for these, ranging from wood, to gold in several colors, with insets of precious stones. Modest, but exquisitely beautiful boxes, covers of memorandum pads and *carnets de bal,* all of which often bore inscriptions, were made of incredibly fine beadwork called *sablé.*

Boxes of the Louis XIV period made of semiprecious stones such as bloodstone or agate mounted in gold, silver or silver-gilt were generally of German or English origin, although the French were using these materials by 1750, if not before. Most snuffboxes of the Louis XV period wore rocaille decorations, whereas oval and round boxes were favored in the Louis XVI period.

Even boxes of inexpensive materials were designed and worked with great skill and taste. In the Louis XV period boxwood was a favorite material for less pretentious pieces, and this extremely hard wood was marvelously carved in arabesques, flowers and an imitation basket weave which required infinite patience and skill. The close fit of the lids of the boxes is remarkable.

During the Louis XV and Louis XVI periods gold boxes had to be stamped by the government controller, so the date of production is definitely established, even when the name of the maker is not available. But in many cases a maker's mark enables one to know that of the goldsmith as well. Four outstanding goldsmiths active between 1735 and 1760 were **Cousinet, Ducrolay, J. F. Breton,** and **Etienne-Lenoir.**

Some silver boxes inlaid with gold were made by the goldsmiths *Le Bastier* and *Robert,* and are of exquisite design and precision.

Less costly, yet very effective boxes were made in *pomponne* or gilded copper, the name for which is derived from the Hôtel Pomponne, where it was first produced. Engraved mother-of-pearl boxes mounted in silver, and *vernis Martin* boxes with gallant scenes and elaborate gold mounts are among the most charming.

Tortoise shell in various forms was used most effectively, sometimes *piqué,* inlaid in gold, sometimes powdered and mixed with color to form a hard paste of brilliant hue which was then inlaid and mounted in gold. This material is known as *poudre d'écaille,* or powdered tortoise shell. The use of three colors of gold was already in vogue in the Louis XV period, but was used more extensively in the reign of Louis XVI. Soft paste porcelain lent itself especially well to articles of small dimensions and boxes were made at Chantilly, Mennecy and Saint-Cloud, in odd shapes of shepherds, shepherdesses, commodes, Chinamen, animals, and a similar variety of forms. Other boxes were

Louis XV Sèvres soft paste snuffbox mounted in gold and studded with diamonds

simply rectangular, but enchantingly decorated with flowers, often on a ground of cross-hatching in the porcelain itself. Most of these were mounted in silver and bear a Paris hallmark.

Boxes of white enamel on copper, embossed in gold and sometimes with colored decoration, were probably made at Saint-Cloud, as they closely resemble the very rare pieces of that factory's porcelain which appear to be jewel-incrusted, so brilliant and clear are their colors. Many less exquisite but nonetheless charming enameled boxes were

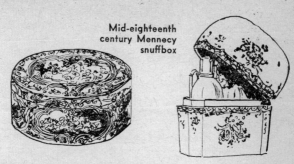

Mid-eighteenth
century Mennecy
snuffbox

Louis XV gold and enamel snuffbox
by Jean George, circa 1755

made in Germany, at Meissen, with *cuivre doré,* gilded
copper mountings. These are mounted in silver with a
Paris hallmark. Some French boxes with enameled bodies
mounted in *cuivre doré* are very attractive, but almost
undistinguishable from those made in Meissen, since the
subjects were often borrowed from each other and the
enamel was quite similar in quality.

A technique perfected in the sixteenth century for painting enamel on gold, became especially popular during the
reign of Louis XVI, when it was widely used for the
decoration of snuffboxes. In this period workmanship
reached its height of perfection and gold boxes with the
most intricate patterns were frequently further enhanced
by the use of three colors of gold. Round and oval boxes
were much in vogue and portraits, cupids and flowers
adorned their lids.

An artist of Flemish origin, **Louis-Nicholas Van Blarenberghe,** painted a series of gouache miniatures which were
mounted in gold to form the top, bottom and sides of
snuffboxes. Perhaps the most famous, is one he painted in
1770 for the Duc de Choiseul showing him surrounded by
his paintings and art treasures in his palace. This is done
with such accuracy that one is able to identify the individual pieces, which are now in museums and famous private
collections. The work of great artists, **Lioux de Savignac,
Jean Joseph Barrière** and **Paul-Nicholas Menière** resembles
that of Van Blarenberghe.

Toward the end of the Louis XVI period tortoise shell boxes with bands of gold decoration were plentiful and still later the tortoise shell was replaced by amboyna wood with a central motif of gilded bronze. These boxes were frequently lined with tortoise shell.

After the Revolution nobles who had escaped the guillotine tried to hide their rank by dressing unostentatiously and carrying less costly snuffboxes of simple material such as wood, ivory, *marquetry de paille* (straw marquetry), and tortoise shell. However, the Empire created a new demand for elaborate boxes, which were often decorated with Napoleon's monogram or portrait and studded with diamonds. Costly gold boxes continued to be the traditional diplomatic gift. During the Restoration some small boxes were made of opaline and plain glass decorated with exquisitely worked paper cut-outs, demonstrating the French ability—apparent throughout her history—to do something charming with the most modest materials whenever she was deprived of more sumptuous ones. Fine French snuffboxes and bibelots are very scarce today and in great demand by many collectors.

CHAPTER TWELVE

Ceramics

The first ceramics made in France are known as *faïence* (or pottery). The word *faïence* became a part of the French language after the introduction of the popular white wares from Faenza, Italy, in the late sixteenth and early seventeenth centuries. While working with faïence the French potters experimented indefatigably to make "true porcelain," but only succeeded after the middle of the eighteenth century.

Faïence was made of rather thick beige or pinkish clay and given a tin glaze composed of fine sand (silica), tin oxides and lead, and an alkali, such as marine salt, potash or soda. Due to the infinitesimal particles of tin oxide, the glaze was white and opaque. Since tin glaze did not run when fired, the decoration could be painted directly on the pottery without danger of being absorbed into the clay and smudged.

Painted tin glaze pottery was made in Mesopotamia as early as the ninth century A.D., and in the tenth by Islamic potters on the southern shores of the Mediterranean, whence it found its way into Spain. When the papal court, established in Avignon in the fourteenth century, employed artists from Italy and Spain, the French artisans learned the "potter's secret" of tin glaze. At that early date floor tiles were being made in green, purple and yellow. Around

1500 Italian potters established themselves in Valencia and Antwerp, introducing the Italian technique of pottery-making into Northern Europe. Some of these men migrated to France around 1530, when, under the direction of Masseot Abaquesne the Rouen factory was established, and made tiles for the floors of churches and châteaux. By 1545 this factory was making apothecary jars in the Italian style. Upon the death of Abaquesne there was a period of inactivity until the tradition of making apothecary jars was revived by Antoine Sigalon.

Early eighteenth
century Rouen
cache pot

In time, the Rouen district became a leading center of faïence production and remained so throughout the seventeenth and eighteenth centuries. Blue and a brownish red were its most charactertistic colors, and typical Rouen designs consisted of medallions, spirals and scrolls in concentric patterns.

All early French faïence was fired at a high temperature known as *grand feu,* but since only a few colors can resist such great heat, the potters were confined to green, blue, purple, yellow and orange. A few factories were able to produce an additional brick red, derived from a special clay or bole, but they were rare exceptions. After firing, the pottery was dipped into a solution of glaze and water and then dried. With the *grand feu* method, the decorations were painted at this stage, on the "raw glaze," the surface of which was still porous. A second firing melted the colors into the glaze and fused it onto the surface of the piece.

The desire for a wider range of color led the potters to experiment with other methods, and around 1750 they were finally able to fire their wares completely before painting them. The colors were then mixed with powdered glass and affixed to the surface of the glaze by a second firing at a much lower temperature, known as *petit feu*. This method made several new shades possible; red and pink, as well as gold leaf.

As early as 1539, **Bernard Palissy,** who spent years of heartbreaking trial and error in a futile attempt to make porcelain, reached unsurpassed heights in the field of faïence. His highly colored pieces with fruit, flowers, animals and sometimes human figures in relief were extremely realistic. He developed the most extraordinary enamel, and his glaze was so transparent that it left the modeling of his pieces as sharply defined as they had been before it was applied. After working many years at Saintes, Palissy's work attracted royal attention, and in 1563, under the protection of the queen-mother, Catherine de Medici, he started a pottery factory near the Louvre.

For a brief period, between 1524 and 1563, a factory at **Saint-Porchaire** made delicate and intricate structures which were miniature replicas of the architecture of the period. These pieces usually on a cream or beige ground with designs primarily in black or brown, are astonishing feats of skill. At the summit of some of their elaborate edifices there is a slight depression for the dramatic and worthy presentation of the highly prized commodity—salt.

Around 1570 a reaction set in against the over-decorated pieces then in vogue and a new form of tableware, called *bianchi di Faenza* or in French, *faïence blanche,* was introduced. When Henri III visited Lyon in 1582 and 1584, the new white faïence was used at banquets arranged for his entertainment. The new ware, which was almost all white with perhaps a crest in blue, yellow and orange on the rim or center of each piece, was quickly accepted in France. The Nevers factory, founded in 1602 under the direction of an Italian potter, Augustin Conrade,

Seventeenth century
Nevers faïence case,
circa 1650

specialized in this type of household ware. A light, cobalt blue ground with white or colored decoration was another product of the factory.

At **Mouistiers** in 1679, Pierre Clérissy directed a faïence factory which utilized designs by such eminent artists as André-Charles Boulle and Jean Bérain. The latter's graceful arabesques and grotesques were often surrounded by a border of conventional scrolls. Soft greens and yellows characteristic of some of the Mouistiers products, are a refreshing change from the all-too-frequent blue and white.

Eighteenth century
Mouistiers tray,
circa 1746

A brother, Joseph Clérissy, founded a factory at **Marseilles** where the Bérain style was also followed for a time by Joseph Fauchier. From 1748 until 1793 this factory was conducted by the widow of Claude Perrin, who signed her work "V.P." (Veuve Perrin). She borrowed some designs from Jean Pillement and was assisted by her business partners, Honoré Savy and Joseph Gaspard Robert. However, it was her taste which dominated the factory's work, and she was responsible for some of the most beautiful pieces ever produced. Her fruits and flowers were painted with delightful freedom, extraordinary balance and a light touch. The ground of most of her pieces was white, but the rare examples with a yellow ground are ravishingly beautiful.

One of the most important faïence factories was **Strasbourg,** founded by the Hannong family in 1721. Charmingly rocaille tableware, decorated with vivaciously painted flowers, often in a purplish red, bright green, light blue and yellow was produced there. The Strasbourg faïence greatly influenced the style of pottery in Germany, Sweden and Hungary, as well as in France. The factory, so successful during two generations, eventually fell into debt, was

Strasbourg wall
cistern and basin
by Paul Hannong

Strasbourg plate with J. H. mark
(Joseph Hannong)

mismanaged in the third and came to an end in 1780. Paul Hannong marked much of the best of his work with his well-known initials: "P.H.," between 1739 and 1760. His son Joseph Hannong used "I.H." between 1762 and 1780.

Sinceny which was established in 1738, made decorations in blue after engravings, and used a border of polychrome foliage. Its charming and extremely popular *chinoiserie* pieces are often confused with those of Rouen if the factory's mark of an "S" is not found.

Sceaux was founded in 1735, but produced little of note until after 1750. It followed the best work of other factories, especially the porcelain shapes of Sèvres. The painting in various shades of crimson "purple of Cassius," green, a vivid blue and gold, was of high quality and the Sceaux products are as fine as any of those made at Niderviller or Strasbourg.

Lunéville in Lorraine, was in operation as early as 1723 and its earliest wares consisted of *grand feu* busts and recumbent lions for garden ornaments. Later pieces attributed to Lunéville were in the Strasbourg Rococo style. The colored flowers in relief and the yellowish tint of the glaze point to this factory but might well have been made at **Saint Clément,** which was situated only eight miles away, was founded in 1758 by Jacques Chambrette of Lunéville, with which it maintained close ties for some time. Later, Saint Clément specialized in almost all-white faïence with gilding as its only decoration. These factories as well as **Les Islettes** where Lunéville potters introduced the *petit feu* technique around 1785, continued well into the first quarter of the nineteenth century. During the Empire period Les Islettes specialized in popular themes such as scenes from the wars, gallant soldiers with their sweethearts, landscapes, flowers and *chinoiserie.*

In the sixteenth century as trade with the Orient developed, hard paste porcelain from China and Japan began to appear on the European market. Its pure white translucence was far superior to even the best faïence and European potters tried many methods of making "true porcelain." One attempt led to the use of *terre de pipe* or pipe clay, called *terre de Lorraine,* in the eastern part of France. It was similar to the clay used for English salt glaze and cream-colored ware. Eighteenth-century French faïence, while imitating porcelain, achieved a special charm and beauty through the wide range of colors which the *petit feu* method of firing had made possible. The soft tin glaze gave it warmth and the exquisite painting of very high artistic quality more than compensated for the clumsier material which they had learned to handle so expertly.

Niderviller, founded in 1754, made unusual pieces of *terre de Lorraine* under the direction of Paul Louise Cyfflé. The Niderviller factory specialized in charming flower painting and figures in the Watteau and Boucher styles, frequently in crimson or iron-red monochrome. These were known as *faïences fines.* The painter Deutsch, working there from 1773 until 1778 used *trompe l'oeil* prints

Niderville tray,
circa 1774

fastened with a nail on a wooden background, as the decoration of plates and platters.

The **Pont au Choux** factory, which was established in Paris in 1743, used pipe clay to make its beautiful rocaille models for silver tureens, sauceboats, salt cellars, mustard pots and other table appointments. Also in Paris, **Bourg-la-Reine,** founded in 1773 and **Aprey** in 1780, produced very fine wares. The **Creil** factory, which dates from 1780 used a light clay similar to that of Pont au Choux and developed a technique of printing under the glaze. This was done in brown, black and red and subjects were borrowed from mythology, religion, contemporary history, rural and urban scenes. The pieces with a yellow ground dating from around 1825 are very attractive.

In 1786 France and Britain signed a commercial treaty which permitted English pottery to enter France with only a nominal duty. This distressed the *faïenciers* so much that they formed a corporation to protest the ruling, which would close some two-hundred-and-forty factories and create about thirty-two-thousand unemployed. The protest was not heeded by the government and a deluge of English salt glaze, Queen's Ware and Leeds cream-colored ware crossed the channel. As these were less expensive than faïence, lighter to transport and less liable to chip or crack under heat, they greatly appealed to the less affluent. English potters joined the Pont au Choux factory in Paris and what the imported wares failed to do to ruin the faïence industry in France was completed by the home product. By 1800 there were very few household faïence factories left.

Faïence reached its highest development in France between 1709 and 1780, and by 1850 the industry was practically extinct. However, because of the charm of the old designs and coloring there is still a certain demand for table services and ornaments, and some factories, including Rouen, Montpellier, Lunéville and Mouistiers are now making reproductions of their former products.

Before they had learned to make "true porcelain" in Europe, the French developed a soft paste which was creamy-white, vitreous and translucent. There is a difference of opinion as to the date this was first discovered, but it appears to have been near the end of the seventeenth century. Some authorities state that *pâte tendre* was invented around 1672 at Rouen, probably by Louis Poterat; it is also known to have been produced by Pierre Chicanneau at Saint-Cloud shortly after that. At first the formula

St. Cloud pastille burner, circa 1750

was a closely guarded secret and production was tremendously hampered thereby, but as workmen moved from one factory to another, the knowledge gradually spread. Soft paste is extraordinarily beautiful and lends itself to the most exquisite decoration and to colors which seem to melt right into the paste—an effect never produced in any other ware. However soft paste was difficult to handle and larger pieces frequently became lopsided in firing. It was also very expensive to make and therefore was mainly used for small pieces, ornamental objects and for deluxe tea and coffee services.

Hard paste porcelain did not become possible in Europe until 1709 when, by a fortunate accident, Johann Friedrich Boettger discovered the indispensable ingredient, kaolin, in Meissen, Saxony. It was not found in France until 1769 when it was discovered at Saint Yrieix, near Limoges. After the Germans had succeeded, the French potters continued to experiment in making hard paste porcelain. It was this ambition which brought financial difficulties to many factories and bankruptcy to Strasbourg in 1780.

The **Saint-Cloud** factory was started around 1678 by

Pierre Chicanneau, who began to work with soft paste porcelain around 1695. Between 1702 and 1715, Saint-Cloud was under the patronage of Louis XIV and the earliest marked pieces bear his emblem, a radiant sun. At the death of Chicanneau, his widow married Trou, who continued the production of soft paste, marking his wares with an incised "St.C." above the letter "T."

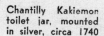

Chantilly Kakiemon toilet jar, mounted in silver, circa 1740

Chantilly, established in 1725, under the protection of Louis-Henri de Bourbon, Prince de Condé, made, among other designs, soft paste copies of Japanese, so-called Korean designs, in the Kakiemon style. Ciquaire Cirou directed Chantilly at its founding and continued as its head until his death in 1751, after which the factory passed through many hands until it went out of business at the end of the century. The smooth, beautiful, milky-white glaze of Chantilly is unique in soft paste porcelain, but little of artistic value was produced after 1780. A red hunting horn is the mark found on pieces made during the best period. At the end of the century the same mark appears in blue.

In 1734 the factory known as **Mennecy** was established by Louis-François de Neufville, Duc de Villeroy on the rue de Charonne. This was the first faïence and porcelain factory in Paris. In 1748 it moved to Mennecy and in 1773 was transferred to Bourg-la-Reine, both in the environs of Paris. The mark "D.V." standing for Duc de Villeroy is sometimes found in red or blue, but is more often incised in the paste on the underside of the piece.

The initials "D.C.P." are also found occasionally. The first manager of this factory was François Barbin, who was later joined by his son, Jean-Baptiste. After their death the factory was directed by Joseph Jullien and Symphorion Jacques in conjunction with one at Sceaux.

Sceaux flower pot, circa 1770

Although in a sense imitative of the work done at Saint-Cloud and Chantilly, Mennecy soft paste acquired a character distinctly its own. The paste at its best was milky-white with a brilliant and often slightly wavy glaze. Flowers and Kakiemon decorations were painted in very soft, but lively colors with pinks and blues predominating and the edges of plates and other pieces were often rose pink or even a brilliant blue. Fruit with a branch and a few leaves formed knobs and handles. Figures were beautifully molded, sometimes after Boucher, or of oriental inspiration and are among the finest ever made. Biscuit was made at Mennecy, as well as at Sèvres, and in some cases the Mennecy biscuit was subsequently glazed at Bourg-la-

Eighteenth century Mennecy figurines mounted as candelabra with soft paste flowers

Reine. The best Mennecy porcelain was produced during the reign of Louis XV; later pieces, sometimes equally well executed, lack the interest and charm of the earlier period.

The **Vincennes** factory is said to have come into existence in 1738 when Giles and Robert Dubois, who had left Chantilly, declared that they possessed the secrets of porcelain making. They were engaged by Orry de Fulvy a nobleman and an amateur of ceramics, who housed them in the disused royal château of Vincennes, near Paris. In 1741 the Dubois brothers, who were heavy drinkers, were discharged and François Gravant, who had also come from Chantilly, replaced them. Gravant claimed to have learned all the Dubois' secrets while they were under the influence of liquor.

Eighteenth century Vincennes soft paste bowl

The factory's first outstanding accomplishment was the modeling and decoration of exquisite porcelain flowers which were handled with such delicacy and taste as to be far superior to those made at Meissen. These were used in conjunction with gilded bronze mounts on clocks, sconces, inkstands and girandoles. They were also used in relief on vases of the same porcelain.

In 1745 a stock company was formed in which Louis XV took a great interest, buying up shares until he finally owned the whole enterprise himself. The chemist Jean Hellot, the goldsmith and sculptor Duplessis, and the enameler Mathieu were engaged to supervise composition, modeling and decoration, while Hulst was made adviser on style. The production of paste and glaze were under the direction of François Gravant until his death in 1765, when he was succeeded by his son, Louis-François. The factory was allowed to use the royal monogram of two interlaced "Ls" accompanied by little flowers or dots. When Vincennes became *Manufacture Royale de Porcelaine* in 1753, this became the official factory mark and letters were added to indicate the year. Thus an "A" stood for 1753, "B" for 1754, and so on. Other marks indicated the painter, the originator of decoration, and sometimes the modeler or gilder. In 1756 the factory moved to Sèvres and its wares became known by this name. After the discovery of kaolin in France in 1769 Sèvres began to make hard paste porcelain and the interlaced "L" mark of this period was surmounted by a crown.

Eighteenth century
soft paste
Sèvres *jardinière*

In 1753 tremendous restrictions had been placed on all rival organizations, to the point of forbidding the manufacture anywhere in France, not only of porcelain, but even of white faïence, decorated in color. Other factories were forbidden to use gilding, or any color other than blue for decorations, or to make glazed or biscuit statuettes or ornaments. As some factories were under the protection of powerful nobles, these rulings could not always be enforced, but the royal factory of Sèvres always dominated the porcelain field in France.

The Louis XV style was abandoned at Sèvres in 1774 in favor of neoclassic designs and much of its charm was lost. In this period, soft paste, hard paste and unglazed biscuit, as well as terra cotta figures were made at the same time. The magnificent Sèvres products were always extremely expensive to produce and even with the King's financing, the factory had great financial difficulties.

During the Revolution Sèvres molds were methodically destroyed and on one occasion seven people spent four hours savagely smashing all the souvenirs of *l'ancien ré-gime* they could lay hands on. At the height of the fury in 1793, and again between 1800 and 1813 great quantities of unfinished and imperfect soft paste pieces were sent to England where they were elaborately decorated by independent enamellers and marked with appropriate date symbols. These half-forgeries flooded the market and continue to be a source of great confusion to collectors. Napoleon ordered many pieces of Sèvres glorifying his Empire, and under the direction of Brongniart, hard paste was technically perfected. However the later products were often cold and metallic and less pleasing to the eye than the delicate soft paste.

The **Strasbourg** factory had been experimenting with porcelain as early as 1726, but did not begin manufacturing it until much later. Paul Hannong, son of the founder, began to make hard paste in 1745, but was forced by the director of Vincennes to desist. He thereupon accepted an invitation from Archduke Carl Theodore and moved to Frankenthal where he established a hard paste factory. His son, Joseph Adam Hannong, re-engaged in hard paste manufacture in France in 1766 and made tea and coffee sets, dinner services and statuettes with designs similar to those used on the factory's faïence. Joseph Hannong concentrated on commercial wares which did not conflict with those of Sèvres and the factory survived until 1780.

After the discovery of kaolin on French soil, several porcelain factories were established within the city limits of Paris. The comprehensive term **Vieux Paris** covers their work, all of which was produced after 1770. Many employed former Sèvres workmen and all followed neoclassic Sèvres models and decoration, so that it is difficult to attribute unmarked pieces to a specific factory. Pierre Antoine Hannong of Strasbourg, founded a factory in the faubourg Saint Denis in 1771 which eventually secured the patronage of the Comte d'Artois, brother of Louis XVI. In 1787 this factory finally received official permission to make porcelain, although it had been doing so for some time.

Locré and Russinger at La Courtille (rue Fontaine-au-Roy) and Clignancourt also were begun in 1771; factories at rue Thiroux in 1775 and rue de Bondy in 1780 followed, all of which were under the patronage of royal personages. *Vieux Paris* factories continued to produce through the Empire period and more of their wares are available than porcelains of earlier date. Porcelains in mint condition are extremely difficult to find, but because of their beauty and rarity defects do not deter a collector from acquiring them.

CHAPTER THIRTEEN

Glass

Glass is composed of various ingredients, chief among which is sand or silica. This can be fused alone at a very high temperature, but early glassmakers found that by mixing silica with other ingredients, fusion could be achieved with less heat. As glass cooled after firing, it was molded into the desired shapes. However, the cooling process had to be retarded by a second firing to prevent the glass from crystalizing and losing its transparency, and if the cooling were too rapid the glass would break from tension.

Glass was known in ancient Egypt, several thousand years before the Christian era; the first known piece having been made between 1551 and 1527 B.C., during the reign of Amenhotep. The earliest specimens were small perfume bottles, amulets, beads and other forms of colored glass jewelry. They were made around a solid nut, which was destroyed after it had been coated with the glass. It was not until the Christian era, when the blowpipe was invented, probably by the Phoenicians, that establishment of the glass industry became possible, and colorless glass was produced for the first time.

Glass, imported from the East, was in common use in France in the early Christian era. Glass vessels have been found in Merovingian tombs, but experts cannot differentiate between it and glass of the Carolingians. Oriental workshops established in France were eventually taken over by native Frenchmen and glass has been produced uninterruptedly ever since the Gallo-Roman period. The first center of the industry was in the Rhône valley and it later moved to the region of Lyon and north to Amiens, Rheims and into Belgium and Germany.

Colored glass imitations of precious stones, sometimes called *cabochons,* were made so perfectly as to fool even an experienced eye and were used side by side with semi-precious stones. Metal altarpieces in churches and all forms of ecclesiastical appurtenances such as chalices, monstrances, reliquaries, crosses, alms plates, and even priests' robes were incrusted with tiny glass cubes affixed with mortar. Imitation stones incrusted in gold were also made for buttons, belt buckles, sword hilts, clasps and other articles of adornment. The Church was the best customer of the early French glassmakers, and it is not surprising that before long some monasteries absorbed the trade and became manufacturers themselves.

Flat glass in brilliant colors was made for the windows of churches at a very early date. It was regarded as a French specialty and in the year 675 Bishop James Wilfred of England requested French glassmakers to make windows for the Cathedral of York. A single, monumental figure was used in the earliest windows, but around the middle of the twelfth century small medallions began to appear. The medallions were interspersed with squares, lozenges and quatrefoils held within an iron framework which itself was a part of the design. The round or rose window was also introduced at this time, and the west front of the cathedral of Chartres which was built at the end of the twelfth century, is the best surviving example.

French glass factories were originally established in forests where the necessary ingredients and fuel could be found. The best sand for glassmaking was found at Fontainebleau, where there were also many ferns. Ferns played a very important role in French glassmaking since they absorbed the potash in sand and produced a very light, greenish glass known as *verre de fougère,* or fern glass.

During the thirteenth century glassmaking in France reached great artistic heights and many windows were made for chapels, halls and rooms of the well-to-do. These were frequently elaborately painted and gilded with scenes depicting episodes in legends, by a technique which later came to be known as *eglomisé*. From contemporary pictures and an occasional mention in ancient books, we have ample proof that glass was in general use, especially for tableware. Various styles of stemmed fern glasses were used by all classes, but only a single drinking glass of the period, conserved at the Musée des Antiquités at Rouen, has survived.

In Lorraine, in the forest of Darney, the manufacture of window glass was monopolized by four families who had emigrated from Bohemia in the fourteenth century. The original document according them special privileges had been burned, but new ones issued in 1469 and 1526, proclaimed the families to be "nobles of the race" in the Duchy of Lorraine. They paid only nominal taxes, had the right to hunt and fish, and to circulate their products without restriction; and were ennobled, despite the fact that they actually worked at their trade. Their exact rank has been much debated and is subject to different interpretations, but the glass-making gentlemen wore swords and embroidered hats and formed a special social caste. Even their assistants were treated as gentlemen rather than ordinary workmen.

In Normandy four other families, originally from Picardy, held a monopoly for the production of bottles, drinking glasses and other small and medium-sized pieces. The process of making window glass in discs, which were later cut into squares, was apparently introduced there prior to 1302 by Philippe Caquerel, a member of one of the families. The almost complete disappearance of gold due to continuous war and the resultant misery, stimulated the production of glass and pewter at a rapid pace.

Glass played an important role in the economic life of the country, and one gauge of a man's wealth was the amount of glass he possessed. The inventory of the Duc d'Anjou's effects in 1360 includes many glass stones which were studded in crowns, figures of saints, reliquaries, receptacles and boxes. Charles VI in 1399 wore a crown of gold which had an imitation emerald in every floral device of its design.

New manufacturing techniques were added in the fifteenth century and factories cropped up rapidly in all forests where the supply of fern and wood was prolific. During the second half of the fifteenth century window glass was of several different shades. Varieties of blue, purple, crimson and, less frequently, green and yellow, were achieved by superimposing different layers of color; and uncolored glass was much closer to white than had heretofore been possible. Although a long time elapsed before people of modest means could afford glass for windows, its use was already widespread among the affluent. Windows remained very narrow until the sixteenth century, when François I had those of the Louvre enlarged for a reception of Charles V of Spain.

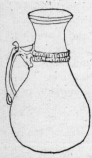

Heavy glass jug of the fifteenth century from Languedoc

The stemless glass or goblet was introduced in the fifteenth century. It was sometimes fluted or spiral and gradually became taller, until toward the end of the century it became a beaker which in various qualities, was used by all classes of society. These glasses were sometimes fluted or spiral in shape. Two or three people drank from one glass, which was not left on the table, but removed to a sideboard where it was refilled. A book on etiquette advised people to hold a glass in one hand only and not to talk while holding it. It also suggested that the glass should not be too large to be drained in one draft, so as not to be unpleasant for the next person using it. For the same reason it was etiquette to wipe one's mouth very carefully on the tablecloth or a napkin before drinking. It was also good form to hold the flat base of the glass with three fingers, two under and the thumb on top, a custom which continued until the end of the eighteenth century. Bottles and glasses of strange shapes were made at this time, as well as lamps, *coupes,* platters, goblets, mugs, pitchers and basins, and all manner of household articles, some of which were occasionally mounted in gold or silver. Glass imitating opal, jasper and agate appeared in 1416; yellow, and painted or enameled glasses were made after 1425.

The nobility imported fine glassware from Venice and a white glass of great brilliance, which they called *le cristallin,* or crystal, appeared at this time. As soon as the necessary ingredients could be found, the French imitated it. Henri II established a deluxe glass factory at Saint-Germain-en-Laye in 1551, in which the Queen, Catherine de' Medici, was tremendously interested, and he proudly announced that the factory was producing wares of the same beauty and excellence as those which the Court was importing from Venice. The industry expanded rapidly and there were more than two thousand workshops by the end of the century. Those of Lyon and Nevers were outstanding, and in Lorraine and Normandy flat glass was being made in increasing quantities. In 1597 Henri IV expressed his satisfaction that the glass industry was able to supply the whole realm; a great deal of it from Lyon and Nevers.

Glass of the second
half of the sixteenth
century (Lorraine type)

In the east of France the desire to establish glass factories in Macon had met with severe opposition from the citizens, who argued that the tax-exempt glassmakers increased their own burdens and were a menace to the town by consuming quantities of wood and depriving the inhabitants of necessary fuel. They also objected to contamination of the air with smoke from the furnaces which invited contagious diseases and the pestilence. This opinion was not shared by the King's representative and the glass factories obtained the necessary authorization to proceed.

Mazarin supported Italian glassmakers, who held monopolies in Nevers, Poitiers and all the cities adjacent to the Loire, for the production of glass and crystal in the Venetian manner. They refused to employ or instruct Frenchmen in their methods and even went to the extent of locking themselves in when blowing glass. It was not until the seventeenth century that the French learned their secrets. In the Paris region a monopoly was held by a Jean Maréchal, who had obtained it through the assistance of the *valet de chambre* of Henri IV.

Sixteenth-century glasses had a short foot sometimes of openwork, and their sides were often fluted. Although output was tremendous and the price very low, it is curious

Golblet of the second half of the sixteenth century from Lorraine

Seventeenth century glass bottle found in the ruins of St. Basil Abbey, Champagne

that several people still drank from one glass in the house of the average citizen. Bottles were not yet used for the transportation of wine, but were filled from storage barrels. The potter Bernard Palissy in 1575, deplored the way glasses and bottles were hauled about by street vendors, who carried their wares in baskets on their backs and on their arms, as though they were selling old hats or old iron!

By 1665, the King and his minister, Colbert, ceased to take any interest in the production of shaped glass, which was so firmly established as to require no special protection. They completely reversed former policy, cancelled all previously accorded monopolies and encouraged even outsiders in the manufacture of mirrors in the Venetian manner. Many mirror factories sprang up, all accumulating debts, until Louis XIV instructed Pontchartrain, the General Controller of Finance, to arrange for an incorporation of all these failing companies under the title of *Manufacture royale des glaces de France*. Even with this august protection, difficulties were encountered, and Saint-Gobin and Tourlaville were obliged to bank their fires. The production of mirrors was then incorporated into a single, state controlled unit which from 1693 on was known as **Saint-Gobin.**

In 1687 **Bernard Perrot** of Orléans announced to the Academy of Science his invention of "a method of pouring the crystal sheets as one poured metal, giving it any desired color; also a means of engraving it with figures, letters and all sorts of decoration, including portraits." The first four mirrors "poured" at la Grenouillère in Paris (the spot presently occupied by the Gare d'Orsay), were presented to Louis XIV in 1691. The first large mirrors were so expensive and so highly valued that Saint-Simon related the case of the Comtesse de Fiesque who sold a tract of wheat-growing land, which she considered uninteresting property, in order to purchase a fine mirror. In 1702 the King intervened for the fifth time and the industry was once more reorganized; this time on a solid footing which enabled it to survive throughout the eighteenth century.

The mirror industry was greatly advanced by the style inaugurated by the architect Robert de Cotte, who became Director of Royal Buildings in 1708. Lowering the chimney pieces in all rooms he designed, de Cotte surmounted them with mirrors and added more mirrors in the panels. Entire rooms were designed with mirrors; the *Galerie des Glaces* in the Palais de Versailles being one of the first examples. Between 1667 and 1695 Louis XIV spent about three-hundred-and-seventy-six-thousand livres on mirrors to decorate the royal palaces of Versailles, Meudon, Fontainebleau, Marly and the Louvre. Those for Versailles were still produced by the old method of blowing glass, but all the others were poured.

Three seventeenth century drinking glasses

Glasses of German design and form were imitated in France at this time but found relatively little favor, whereas their liqueur and perfume bottles were very popular. Simple lines seem to have pleased the French better than complicated Italian forms, but they nevertheless liked drinking glasses in the shape of animals, clocks, boats, church steeples and similar fancies.

A contemporary journal states that Louis XIII played in his childhood with a glass dog and other animals made at Nevers. Earrings, chains, painted figurines and many charming bibelots were produced at the same time, but no existing pieces can be attributed undisputably to the seventeenth century. This famous spun and painted glass of Nevers was made under shockingly unhealthy conditions, for the dim lamps of the workmen were fed with inexpensive horse fat which gave off choking fumes and as a result, workers were ill most of the time, and died prematurely.

In 1727 a glass factory was established at Sèvres under the name, *Verrerie Royale de Sèvres*. It was presented to

Early eighteenth century Nevers opaline flaçon with ball stopper and polychrome enamel decoration

White Nevers glass flaçon, polychrome enamel decoration, circa 1710

Madame de Pompadour by Louis XV in 1750, and in 1755 moved to Bas-Meudon to prevent its fumes from damaging the porcelains being made at Sèvres.

Eighteenth century fern drinking glass

There was a revival of interest in long-neglected fern glass in the eighteenth century when a group of sophisticated men decided it enhanced the flavor of wine. A number of factories were making cut and uncut crystal in the Bohemian style which was very popular throughout the last quarter of the eighteenth century. Glass in the English manner known as "flint glass" was made in France for the first time in 1772, but quantities of it were still being imported from England. Because of its clarity it was particularly popular for chandeliers, lanterns, drinking glasses and optical supplies. The first French flint-glass factory, which used English workmen, was established in 1783 near the park of Saint-Cloud. In the following year, having obtained the patronage of Marie Antoinette, it was called *Manufacture des Cristaux et Emaux de la Reine*. The factory depended upon coal for its fuel and so moved to Montcenis in order to be near its source of supply.

An adequate fuel supply had always been a serious problem for the glass industry and as wood became increasingly scarce, the government placed mounting restrictions on its use. In consequence, many glassmakers began to burn peat or coal and moved to the ports where they would have easy access to this fuel, much of which had to be imported from England. Many glass factories were able to survive the expensive transition only by lowering their artistic standards and turning to the manufacture of household articles.

The discovery that wine kept longer in a glass bottle than any other container was a great boon to the glass in-

dustry. It is said that champagne owes its life to this
discovery, for it was observed that the sooner wine was
bottled after the harvest, the more of its sparkle remained.
Champagne was said to be unfailingly perfect if bottled
between the tenth and fourteenth day of the March moon.

"Black glass" bottles, in imitation of the English variety,
were manufactured by the thousands in the beginning of
the eighteenth century. Around 1700 the wine bottle had a
bulbous, onion shape, which later became elongated and
cylindrical. Bottles were supposed to hold a prescribed
amount of liquid, in four standard sizes. However, bottle-
makers were suspected of having an agreement with the
wine merchants to make bottles which contained somewhat less than the legal amount. To foil this practice, a
law was passed forbidding the sale of already-bottled
wine, and making it mandatory for merchants to measure
the wine into pewter vessels which had been approved by
the authorities and marked accordingly.

Bluish glass bottles of very charming appearance were
manufactured in Languedoc and sometimes used for oil.
Others were used in apothecary shops, and for mineral
water. From 1799 on, Lyon delivered bottles expressly
for the transportation of Vichy water to Paris. Other food-
stuffs were also packed in glass for exportation during the
second half of the eighteenth century.

Even as late as the eighteenth century, drinking glasses
were not left on the table during meals, so no complete
glass services were made. However, individual drinking
glasses were fashioned in various sizes, depending on
whether they were to be used for *le vin ordinaire* (domes-

Late Louis XVI goblet

tic wine), *le vin étranger* (imported wine), for *liqueurs*
or for *l'eau-de-vie* (brandy). There were three sizes, designated as large, medium and small, in each of these types.
Glasses were also made to special order and painted with

people's names, little verses and amorous sentiments, for a specific person or occasion, such as an engagement, marriage, birth or baptism, as well as for gifts.

In the eighteenth century the Nevers factory was responsible for the many extraordinary little spun-glass painted figurines, grottos, crêches (scenes of the Nativity), cosmetic jars, toilet accessories and countless charming odd bits for household use. The milky painted glass is known as "opaline," a type which was extremely popular but far less artistic in the early nineteenth century.

In the nineteenth century the site of a glass factory was dictated by its fuel requirements, so the owners sought proximity to the supply of coal, to the railroads and to the canals. Baccarat and Saint-Louis remained in the eastern part of France, where it was easier to recruit skilled labor; others preferred to be near their outlets and settled close to the gates of Paris and Lyon, where they were able to sell all of their wares without a transportation problem. Amongst the mirror factories, Saint-Quirin continued to use wood as fuel, and in 1819 Saint-Gobain purchased another forest so as to make sure of having a supply of the fuel which they were accustomed to burn.

Then, as a result of new discoveries in chemistry, artificially produced ingredients began to be used instead of the old ones.

The Revolution abolished all privileges formerly accorded special factories, and all who wished to produce glass were obliged to compete in the open market for their required raw materials and for the wood which they had formerly enjoyed as privileged citizens. The wood-burning factories decreased in number as coal became the major fuel of the nineteenth century.

During the Empire period and the succeeding years, flint glass of heavy quality and heavy forms was much in vogue and continued so throughout the first half of the nineteenth century. Opaline (milky glass) with colorful painted decorations was extremely popular, and especially so in the new and varied shades of blue during the Restoration and the reign of Charles X. Nineteenth-century glass suffered from the same decadence in taste which affected all other French crafts and it is unfortunate that

pieces of this period—which have little more than quaintness to recommend them to a collector—are more easily
found than the utterly charming earlier products.

PART FOUR

CHAPTER FOURTEEN

Ébénistes

The following biographical notes on some of the great artisans of French furniture are based to a great extent on information gathered from the splendid book on French cabinetmakers of the eighteenth century written by the late Comte François de Salverte.[1] Since his great work is contained in a very large volume, I have selected a number of cabinetmakers whose influence on the history of furniture has made their names famous or familiar. The fact that I have been obliged to select only a few of the many worthy of mention and have considerably condensed information covering them does not mean that a cabinetmaker not discussed here was of lesser caliber or ability. In the interest of brevity I have eliminated a great many whom I should have liked to include and whose works are of great interest and beauty.

André-Charles Boulle, celebrated cabinetmaker in the Louis XIV period was born in Paris in 1642 where he died in 1732. The son of a cabinetmaker of artistic pieces, he was highly gifted, showing unusual aptitude for all forms of decoration. André-Charles Boulle devoted himself in his youth to design, painting and sculpture and showed such ability that he was later received as a mem-

---

[1] François de Salverte, *Les Ébénistes Du XVIII⁰ Siecle, Leurs Oeuvres et Leurs Marques,* Vanoest, Les Editions D'Art et D'Histoire, Paris, 1953.

ber of the Academy of Saint Luke. In 1664 he established himself as a free workman under the franchise of the University, in a shop belonging to the College of Reims, where he practiced painting and marquetry. In this latter capacity he soon surpassed all his rivals and was only thirty years of age when Colbert described him to the King as the "most capable in Paris" and was instrumental in having him housed in the gallery of the Louvre. As time went on Louis XIV showered Boulle with marks of favor and named him "first cabinetmaker," qualified and entitled to undertake architecture, painting, sculpture, mosaic, also engraving on metal and the invention of monograms. As a guest of the Sovereign he was free of the restraint of his guild which prohibited a man from exercising more than one of these professions and was thus enabled to work in metal as well as in wood, with a staff of assistants including twenty cabinetmakers and some of the best workers in bronze of the period.

The years that followed his installation in the Louvre were the most brilliant of his career. The administrative correspondence and accounts of the period bear witness to the importance of Boulle's role in the vast projects Louis XIV undertook in the transformation and embellishments of the Royal palaces. Attached to the Service of Buildings he undertook the entire decoration of such rooms as the Jewel Cabinet of the Grand Dauphin at Versailles. His contemporaries considered this the most outstanding curiosity in the palace and the masterpiece of the artist. At this same time he furnished the Crown with a vast profusion of cupboards, desks, commodes, cabinets, and marquetry clock cases, as well as gilded bronze chandeliers and girandoles. He even made chairs inlaid with tortoise shell and brass. Magnificent pieces were ordered by the King and Queen, the Duc and Duchesse d'Orléans, le Grand Condé and the Prince and Princess de Conti. His fame crossed France's frontiers and afterwards the Duc de Lorraine and Savoie, King Philip V of Spain, the Elector of Bavaria, and the Bishop of Cologne, all wanted work by the master. Also the great financiers and men of high position vied with each other for his products and paid huge sums to obtain them.

However, despite his great success, Boulle was never without financial worries, due in large part to the tardiness with which his clients paid him. Added to those difficulties he was obsessed with the collector's mania, and bought paintings, prints and objects of art without consideration of their cost. He borrowed money right and left in order to satisfy his artistic cravings and incurred debts of huge proportions. Even the intervention, threats, and the grace of the King did not curb his extravagances and he owed money to everyone, including his employees, whom he was unable to pay. On August 19, 1720, to complete the disaster, a fire consumed his workshop, destroying the wood which he had there for his work, his models, a quantity of his finished work, and the major part of his collections. Despite his advanced age he had the courage and the energy to restore his establishment, which he continued to conduct with astonishing vigor until his ninetieth year.

During his long period of activity Boulle varied his style very little. One can barely distinguish the tendency of his earlier work toward classicism and architectural forms from that of later date which tended toward greater lightness and grace. Influenced by LeBrun, Bérain and Robert de Cotte, Boulle designed his furniture himself and may be considered the founder of the traditions on which the school of French furniture making is based.

Strangely enough, the style of brass and shell inlay to which his name is attached was not invented by Boulle, but had been practiced in Italy since the end of the sixteenth century. Examples had been introduced into France by Marie de' Medici and Cardinal Mazarin and were subsequently imitated by Boulle, whose merit lay in the perfection of the art and variation in the use of materials and subject matter for decorations. In some cases, he used plain wood so that the magnificent bronzes he designed would stand out in more dramatic relief.

The fragile nature of the materials Boulle used, such as tortoise shell, horn and metal, made his pieces especially subject to the ravages of temperature changes and humidity, as these materials expand and shrink unequally and adhere to wood with varying degrees of tenacity. Therefore relatively little of his work remains, and since the practice of signing furniture was unknown in his day, it is almost impossible to do more than conjecture which of the remaining pieces is really by his hand. Added to the vicissitudes of climate, there was the vandalism at the time of the Revolution and the fact that Boulle furniture was very much in vogue during the Louis Philippe period, during which it was subjected to horrifying repairs and alterations.

The Louvre has four pieces indisputably by the master. The South Kensington Museum and the Wallace Collection in London and a few others possess pieces of undoubted authenticity.

Of Boulle's seven children, four sons survived to carry on his tradition, and continued to bear the title of "Cabinetmakers to the King." Very little is known about their work except that they continued in their father's footsteps without originality or any perceptible change, usually copying their father's models.

Jean-Philippe, who was born in 1680, died in 1744. He was made a master in 1725 and lodged in the gallery of the Louvre as an *ébéniste, marqueteur, ciseleur et doreur* of his Majesty. The protection of the monarch did not, however, prevent him, a few weeks later, from being arrested and imprisoned at Fontainebleau for his debts. He remained incarcerated until the marriage of Louis XV, when amnesty was granted him.

Pierre-Benoit, born near 1682, ceased to work for his father some time between 1720 and 1725 and settled in the Faubourg Saint-Antoine where he lived a very modest life with an uneducated wife and died without issue in 1741.

Similarly, **André-Charles** who was born in 1685 left the Louvre before the death of his father. His talents as a sculptor had won him a *prix de Rome* at the age of twenty-four and during his attendance at the Academy he formed friendships with a number of artists, such as the painter Parrocel and the sculptor from Antwerp, Michel van der Voort. He derived no advantages from these associations however, since they only led him into bad habits such as gambling, laziness and debauchery. Completely ruined, he was reduced to spending his last days living on the charity of a faithful servant—whom he had neglected to pay for her services for sixteen years. He died in 1745, leaving a host of creditors, among them his old collaborators, who were never able to collect what he owed them for their services.

The last of the four sons, **Charles-Joseph,** called *Boulle le jeune* lived all his life in the gallery of the Louvre where he was born in 1688. After having been associated at first with his father and later with his brother, by 1745 he was the last remaining titular head of his father's workshop. He rented a part of the lodgings which he had as a royal concession, to the *ébéniste* **J. F. Oeben,** who was also always in financial distress. Charles-Joseph was violently attacked and wounded by a creditor for the small sum of eighteen livres and in 1754 he died in misery, without issue.

One of the earliest and at the same time one of the greatest *ébénistes* was **Charles Cressent,** (1685–1768) who was the cabinetmaker of the Regent, fastidious Duke Philippe d'Orléans, and the author of some world-famous commodes. The bronzes which he designed himself are as noteworthy as his cabinetwork. Only a few of his later pieces are signed.

Although of the same family, other members who devoted their extraordinary talents to making chairs spelled their name differently. They were **Jacques-Louis, Jean-Baptiste, Louis, Michel,** and **Réne Cresson,** and possibly others whose Christian names and identity are not clear but all of the above were acknowledged amongst the great.

Bernard Van Riesen Burg, is considered to be one of the greatest cabinetmakers of all times. Most of his superb furniture dates from the Louis XV period, and his work was signed with the initials **B.U.R.B.** Until recently he remained anonymous, but a few years ago, after intensive research, the French scholar Jean Pierre Baroli, identified him by finding a scrap of paper in the archives with the full signature of this great master of Dutch origin. Although three generations of the same family bore the same name and used the initials, we are primarily interested in **Bernard Van Riesen Burg, the Second.** His father who worked in the *Grande Rue du faubourg Saint-Antoine* acquired his master's degree before 1722, and died in 1738. Bernard the Second became a master before 1730 and it is to him that we owe the most splendid of the pieces with that signature. His son, **Bernard the Third** never qualified as a master officially, which would presumably have been an unnecessary formality since he continued to work under his father and to carry on the family tradition, which by then was well known. Bernard the Third died in 1800. The most marked characteristic of B.U.R.B. furniture is the use of dark wood or *bois de bout* (wood taken across the grain) to outline motifs and to form the naturalistic marquetry flowers; he never used colored woods. The dark wood on the light *bois de rose* background outlines the bronze mounts which were made to conform with the marquetry arabesques. B.U.R.B.'s commodes in the pure Louis XV style are *bombé* and generally have two drawers without any dividing line between them. The front panel is treated as a single unit with its design covering both drawers as though there were only one, and the drawer handles are worked into the pattern without disturbing its harmony.

Three generations of the **Migeon** family are also of great interest, especially the work of **Pierre II** whose magnificent use of the pattern in the grain of the woods he employed, created a special type adapted by only a few of his most painstaking contemporaries, such as **Nicholas Jean Marchand,** born in 1697 and made maître before 1738, and a little-known *ébéniste* named **J. Manser,** whose cabinet is reproduced in the illustrated edition of Count de Salverte's famous book. *Bois de violette* seems to have been the most suitable wood for this treatment.

Criaerd or **Criard** was the name of a Flemish family, several members of whom became cabinetmakers in Paris. **André** flourished during the first half of Louis XV's reign, at the end of which period he had a business connection with Migeon. **Mathieu,** his younger brother, was born in 1689, gained his master's degree on July 29, 1738, and practiced his profession with great ability and success, working for J. F. Oeben, the *ébéniste du Roi*. He specialized in magnificent commodes, some of which are in Chinese lacquer and others in marquetry. His son, **Antoine-Mathieu,** succeeded him and signed his pieces M. Criard at first, then Criard without any initial. After 1771 when he succeeded his colleague **Charles Chevallier** in the Rue du Bac, he frequently used the name of the late owner of that establishment. At least one member of the family made chairs.

The same **Charles Chevallier** whose workshop Criard took over after the owner's death, had worked with Criard's brother Jean Mathieu to produce some magnificent pieces of furniture in *marquetrie à fleurs* richly embellished with elaborate and beautifully designed bronzes. Chevallier was born around 1700; became *maître* before 1738, and died in Paris in 1771. In 1769 he was mentioned in the *Almanach d'Indications* as meriting attention for his splendid furniture of very high quality, decorated with flowers in precious, exotic woods. Even during his lifetime his pieces were acquired avidly by the great of France.

Still another master cabinetmaker of Flemish extraction was **Roger Vandercruse Lacroix,** who signed his work with his initials R.V.L.C. and was among the greatest of his generation. He was born in 1728 and acquired his master's degree in 1755, after which time he succeeded his father in the workshop in the rue du faubourg Saint-Antoine. As a result of the perfection and elegance of his work he soon became fashionable and was commissioned to make an entire suite of furniture for the Countess du Barry at Louveciennes, and other pieces for the Tuileries. His work shows extraordinary refinement of taste, most graceful lines and the finest workmanship, frequently in various colors of wood with a predominance of green-stained sycamore. The bronzes used on his furniture are magnificent in design and quality but very discreet in quantity. Although Louis XV was the reigning monarch during the first quarter of a century of his activity as a cabinetmaker, many of Lacroix's finest pieces are in the Transition style. Reaching the age of seventy-one, he lived through the entire reign of Louis XVI and produced some extraordinary examples of that style. During the Revolution he retired from business but continued to work for his pleasure. The Wallace Collection in London possesses a most exquisite example of his work in the form of a small table with a Sèvres porcelain tray top, the latter dated 1760, with a mark showing that it was painted by Ledoux. This wonderful table has an undershelf in floral marquetry in various colored woods and splendid gilded bronze mounts.

Jacques Dubois (1693–1763) and his sons **Louis** and **René** (1737–1799) were notable Parisian cabinetmakers whose signatures are found on sumptuous commodes and desks, both *bureau plats* and the drop-leaf *dos d'âne* type. Their magnificent work is represented in the Musée du Louvre, the Wallace Collection in London and other notable collections.

Leonard Boudin, born in 1735 of obscure and modest origin rose to fame after the *ébéniste* Migeon commissioned him to execute some marquetry and lacquer furniture for the Marquis de Castelmore and other well-known personalities of the day. So great was his success that he in turn employed some of his distinguished confreres such as **Louis Moreau, Gerard Peridiez** and later **Denizot, Evalde, Gilbert** and **Topino.** His business grew to such dimensions that he had to depend more and more on his collaborators to do the actual cabinetwork, but whatever bears his signature is of excellent taste and quality, as he was a real artist who never allowed his name to be affixed to anything but first-rate pieces.

The great **Antoine Robert Gaudreau,** attached to the service of the Crown between 1726 and his death in 1751, failed to sign his magnificent work, so that only two pieces in existence have been identified as unmistakably by his hand, although the records show that he made many extraordinary pieces for the court.

The **Saunier family** was another which became great cabinetmakers during the reign of Louis XV. It reached the pinnacle of success with **Claude Charles Saunier** whose early works were carried out in the Louis XV style, but who then went on to great heights of imagination and invention in the Louis XVI style and continued to work throughout the latter's reign. In 1799 after the death of his first wife, Saunier closed his workshop.

Nicolas-Jean Marchand, born around 1697, obtained his *maîtrise* before 1738 and made luxury furniture with great success. He is known for his marquetry of high quality and is represented in the Musée de Carnavalet in Paris, the Bibliotheque of the Rue de Sully, and other notable collections.

Jean-François Oeben, born around 1720, died 1763, must be added here in his rightful place as one of the greatest cabinetmakers of the Louis XV period and a protégé of Mme. de Pompadour, who early recognized his talents. When his lease, in the workshop at the Louvre, expired upon the death of his employer, the son of the great Boulle, he obtained the title of *ébéniste du Roi* and was allowed to establish himself at the Gobelin factory. From then on his reputation grew and his fame spread throughout the circles of those who were interested in the development of artistic furniture. A sculptor and an expert at the forge, he was able to design and execute most unusual mechanical devices which allowed him to express his creative genius in fashioning unheard-of pieces. In 1756 Oeben and his brother were again obliged to move due to insufficient space in the Gobelin workshop. They then established themselves in the recently built Arsenal building.

Oeben surrounded himself with the greatest craftsmen of his time—the cabinetmakers Riesener, Leleu and Carlin. Caffieri, the sculptor, worked on the decoration of Oeben's furniture, and the great Duplessis, both father and son, Forestier, Hervieux, Gastellier and Guinard all delivered bronzes for his works which were then gilded by Briquet, Caron, Fagard and Jubert.

After Oeben's untimely death in bad financial condition, his widow, who was the oldest daughter of the cabinet-maker François Vandercruse and sister of the great Roger Vandercruse known as Lacroix, carried on his workshop and continued to use his signature, "J. F. Oeben" on furniture produced there after his death. Riesener, who had worked with Oeben and collaborated with him on the famous *bureau du Roi* (conserved at the Louvre), continued to work there until 1767, in which year Françoise-Marguerite Vandercruse Oeben married Riesener and turned the shop over to his direction.

Oeben's brother Simon, who had worked with Jean-François most of his life and who also became an *ébéniste du Roi,* shared his brother's fate by dying in the prime of life, leaving a destitute widow with five children. Business acumen was not one of the gifted brothers' qualities!

Of German origin, **Jean George Schtichtig** was forty-five years old when he obtained his master's degree in 1765. However, he had a very skillful hand at marquetry and was considered worthy of working for the Royal Family. A commode bequeathed to the Louvre by Comte Isaac Camondo was made for Marie Antoinette, whose initials are encrusted in mother-of-pearl at the corners, while the marquetry, showing architectural perspectives and people in the costumes of the time, was done in ivory and precious woods. The Carnavalet Museum in Paris has another of his commodes, decorated with trophies and bouquets of flowers in very light wood.

Gilles Joubert, famous cabinetmaker of King Louis XV was born in 1689 and died in Paris in 1775. The date he attained his master's degree is unknown as it was probably at the beginning of the Régence period when records were not accurately kept. He married the daughter of a colleague who was a cousin of Pierre Migeon, at that time in high favor with Mme. de Pompadour. Thus his work attracted the attention of the King. The *Garde-Meuble,* the royal furniture warehouse began employing him in 1749. In the same year he finished a little marquetry *secrétaire* which contained a silver writing set furnished by the goldsmith Ballin. Next, he made special game tables for the several games then in vogue, a very fine commode for Mme. Adélaide, and another for Mme. Louise. In 1754 he was commissioned to make an important series of furnishings for the new quarters at the Château de la Muette and, some months later, a pair of sumptuous corner pieces for the *petits appartements* at Versailles. The latter are described in detail in the *Journal du Garde-Meuble National.* Around this same time the artist made a *table volante* for Choisy, under the direction of the engineer Guerin de Montpellier for the little suppers of Louis XV. It was a round table with a border wide enough to hold plates and cutlery for twelve persons. The mobile center section or tray was raised and lowered for each separate course of the meal and four small buffets on the same order supplied the drinks. The mechanical work on this famous table was done by Sulplice, the oak base by Pierre Léchaudelle, *menuisier du Roi* at the Gobelins, and Joubert covered the whole with the most elegant marquetry, further enhanced by bronzes made by the great Forestier. From 1758 on, the Master became the regular accredited cabinetmaker to the *Garde-Meuble* of the Crown, which up to that time he had served only occasionally. In the following period Joubert made two superb tall clock cases for the bedroom of Louis XV at Versailles and other precious pieces of the height of luxury. Upon the death of Oeben, he was appointed to appraise the latter's stock and then inherited the title of *ébéniste du Roi.*

Advancing age seems to have had no slowing effect on Joubert's activity, which increased as time went on. In the last phase of his career he achieved some very rich work for the Petit Trianon which Louis XV had just finished building in honor of Mme. du Barry. He was also commissioned to complete the installation of the Château de Saint-Hubert where the King and the Court lodged during the hunts in the forest of Rambouillet. The Mesdames de France continued to demand magnificent commodes, sometimes in black lacquer, sometimes in *marqueterie à fleurs* with attributes and architectural decoration. For the Dauphine and the Comtesse de Provence Jubert also created precious pieces of furniture, and he continued to work until his eighty-seventh year, when he finally retired in 1774. Joubert signed very few of his pieces and only through research has his authorship of some very fine ones in great collections been definitely established.

Much has already been said about **Jean Henri Riesener,** whose work was the expression of the best and the most typical furniture of the Louis XVI period. Born at Gladbeck, near Essen, Germany, in 1734, he had the good fortune to enter the workshop of the great Jean-François Oeben, the cabinetmaker of the King, where he perfected his unusual talents. He gained his *maîtrise* in 1768 after the death of his master, whose workshop he then took over. The next ten years were the most brilliant and fruitful of his career. The whole Court clamored for his work and his output was so prodigious that he amassed a great fortune.

Seven years after the death of his first wife he married

again, but this proved to be an unfortunate union, fraught with domestic quarrels. In 1785 the King's accountants, alarmed by the precarious condition of the Treasury, demanded itemized accounts and accused him of exorbitant and ridiculous charges. Riesener, convinced of his merits and integrity, took exception to their claims and was incensed at their attitude. He soon realized that this approach had merely been an inept attempt to lower his prices. He was however obliged to sign papers of submission, agreeing to furnish certain household items at fixed prices and to submit estimates in advance on other pieces of a more unusual nature. Although his business had already declined to a small fraction of his previous sales he continued to enjoy the favor of the Queen, who was too great a lady to haggle over prices and also too obsessed by her craving for his beautiful furniture to be influenced by the financial condition of the Treasury. He, therefore, continued to furnish Marie Antoinette with magnificent pieces intended primarily for the *Château de Saint-Cloud*. Two of these are known to have been delivered as late as 1790 and 1791. Riesener's optimism led him to believe that the crisis would only be temporary and when the royal furnishings were sold, he bought back some of his own work in the hope of re-selling it to greater advantage when things had calmed down. Unhappily the Terror lasted longer than he had thought possible and by then his furniture was outmoded as the doctrines of the painter David discredited the Louis XVI style. Appreciated nonetheless by his fellow craftsmen, Riesener was appointed as a judge by the Tribunal of Commerce.

He died at the age of seventy-one in 1806. Although forgotten for a long time after his death, he was re-discovered in the latter part of the nineteenth century by people of taste and was rehabilitated to his deservedly lofty position in the history of the furniture of France.

Denis-Louis Ancellet, who started to work as a free artisan, became a master in 1766 and became a counselor to his corporation during the last years of the Louis XVI period. In the spring of 1791 when Louis XVI was planning to reside at Saint-Cloud, and preparations were being made to receive the Court there, he received huge orders for furniture for the Crown. His signature is found on precious furniture in solid mahogany and on some marquetry pieces of high quality. His name in conjunction with that of Weisweiler on at least one known piece attests to the co-operation of these two great artists.

Martin Carlin, one of France's greatest cabinetmakers and one whose work has long been considered to be among the finest ever produced, died in Paris in 1785. Little is known of his history, but he appears to have been a quiet, serious man, dedicated to his work. He produced some important pieces for Marie Antoinette and for the sisters of Louis XVI. He made sumptuous pieces in solid ebony with Japanese lacquer contrasting exquisitely with the gilded bronze mounts of magnificent quality, generally attributed to Gouthière. His lightness and perfection of design are unique and he is known for his exquisite tables in both *bois de rose* and in mahogany with Sèvres tops and plaques. The Musée du Louvre, the Victoria and Albert Museum and the Wallace Collection in London, as well as the Metropolitan Museum in New York are amongst those fortunate in having examples of the work of this great master.

The son of a cabinetmaker named François Garnier, **Pierre Garnier** was born about 1720 and passed his master's test in 1742 while his father was still active. Celebrated throughout his fifty years of cabinetmaking he is classed as one of the first of his time. His excellent taste and technical skill permitted him to express his ideas in the making of very fine pieces. The Musée du Louvre, South Kensington Museum and many other great collections are the proud possessors of pieces made by Garnier.

Etienne Levasseur, born in 1721, worked in his youth with one of the sons of the great André-Charles Boulle and under his tutelage learned the technique of making Boulle furniture in ebony, inlaid with brass and pewter. He repaired furniture by Boulle and later made originals in the same style, often in such a manner that it is very difficult to be certain which is which. He was commissioned to work for the Crown, the Court, and all of the great of his day, and many of his pieces are still in existence.

Levasseur was the one cabinetmaker of the eighteenth century who knew how to work in the Boulle style. During the nineteenth century these traditions were continued by his son **Pierre-Etienne,** who married the daughter of Roger Lacroix; and then continued by his son **Levasseur Jeune,** during the reigns of Charles X and Louis Philippe. This grandson was commissioned to work for the Queen of Spain, for whom he made some very rich pieces incrusted with lapis lazuli and mother-of-pearl.

Godefroy Dester was received as master on July 27, 1774 and worked in the rue du faubourg Saint-Antoine until 1790. The archives furnish us with no details, but we know that he was a flourishing cabinetmaker whose success was justified by his great taste and talent. He made many small pieces of furniture of charming finesse. His use of *citronnier* (lemon wood) of a beautiful tonality, inlaid with lines of *bois de rose,* is a special feature of his very fine work.

Charles Topino worked as a free cabinetmaker before acquiring his master's degree in 1773. He is famous for his small pieces of furniture such as *bonheurs-du-jour* and his remarkable little tables. His work, full of fantasy and charm reached its height in the small tables which were already highly esteemed during his lifetime and are to be seen in many of the great museums and private collections today.

Nicolas Petit (1732–1791) began to work under Louis XV and continued under Louis XVI until his death in 1791. He was particularly skillful in following the new vogue for the so-called classical lines and showed great ingenuity in adapting himself to the new fashion. He is at his best in his commodes and small tables. His transition period furniture is unusually original and pleasing.

François Gaspard Teuné was born in 1726 and became a master in March 1766. The quality of his work is exceptional, and he specialized in the *bureau à cylindre* (roll-top desk) the most famous of which, made during the reign of Louis XVI for the Comte d'Artois with the arms of France and the count's orders and decorations incorporated in the marquetry, now forms part of the Royal Collection at Windsor Castle.

Philippe Claude Montigny, born in 1734, died in Paris in 1800, and is considered one of the best cabinetmakers of his generation. Son of Louis Montigny, a privileged worker in the faubourg Saint-Antoine, he acquired his *maîtrise* in 1766 and kept the old workshop of his father. He became celebrated for his furniture in the style of Boulle, which came back into style at this period. He was commissioned by the Crown to repair many pieces by the great Boulle, which, by then, were in bad condition. The *Mobilier National* still has a number of these historic pieces which survived the fire of the Tuileries in 1871. One of these is on view in the *galerie d'Apollon* at the Louvre and bears the Montigny stamp in very large letters.

In working so long on the furniture of the old cabinet-makers Montigny absorbed their spirit and technique and made it his own. Some pieces of his own design show great masculinity and imposing elegance, for he was an artist of great taste. Some of his pieces have found their way into collections such as the Jacquemart-André Museum.

Jean-François Leleu, 1728–1807, was one of the most famous cabinetmakers of his age. In his youth he had worked for J. F. Oeben; when Oeben died, he established a workshop of his own and soon became widely known for the unusual quality of his work. He made sumptuous furniture for the Prince de Condé, various nobles, and for Mme. du Barry. Toward the end of the Louis XV reign, he furnished the Court with many things which the *Mobilier National* still possesses. Assuming the responsibility of furnishing entire châteaux and palaces from the reception rooms to the attic, he managed even in the simpler pieces to avoid banality and to impart something special to their construction and decoration.

Denis Genty, notable cabinetmaker, lived in the faubourg Saint-Antoine when he was received as a master in 1754. Later he moved to the *rue de l'Echelle-Saint-Honoré*. He became the rage and counted amongst his clients many of the great names of his day, but he grew involved in financial difficulties by overextending his business and in 1762 was declared bankrupt. His colleague Louis Moreau took over his large stock of furniture, which was of very fine taste and quality and the most charming Louis XV style.

Germain Landrin who was received as a master in 1738 was one of the most ingenious cabinetmakers of his time. He was so modest that he worked for many years as an assistant in the workshops of several of his illustrious colleagues. At first he worked with Migeon who greatly influenced his style, especially in the treatment of wood veneer, using the grain of wood to form the design of his decoration. Later he worked with Genty and with Oeben. He himself possessed the qualities and the ability of a first rate *ébéniste* and never stooped to produce inferior pieces. At times his work is undistinguishable from that of Migeon or Oeben, for all of Landrin's work was of absolutely top quality.

Pierre Rousell, 1723–1782, was a notable furniture maker in Paris. He was the son of an assistant to a cabinet-maker and the oldest of four brothers. Married very young, he acquired his master's degree in 1745 and was honored by his community by being given high posts in 1762, 1777 and 1779 respectively. He exercised his trade at the rue Charenton, modestly at first, but his business grew very large and he enjoyed great success. After he had been elected as arbiter in a legal case between his colleague Grandjean and a commission agent in furniture, he was classed among the first cabinetmakers in Paris. From 1775 on he received orders from the Prince de Condé for the Palais Bourbon and the château at Chantilly. Through the little fortune that this brought him he was able to marry his two daughters into the families of petty government officials. He also had two sons who became his pupils and assistants. Pierre Rousell died very suddenly at the age of fifty-nine. The very considerable inventory of his merchandise, which was made by the cabinetmakers Leleu and Cochois, attests to the prosperity of his workshop. There were over fifty commodes of all types, and tables in marquetry, mosaic, woods from the Indies, lacquer and mahogany. His widow carried on the establishment with the help of her sons. Both acquired their masters' degrees and the older, **Pierre Michel** opened a sort of branch workshop especially dedicated to making deluxe furniture. He continued to enjoy the favor of the Prince de Condé and became one of the official furnishers to the Court.

The very fine pieces bearing his signature, the earliest of which are in the pure Louis XV style were very likely made during the father's lifetime. Others in the Louis

XVI style were probably made by the sons, who continued to use the father's stamp and to work until the end of the monarchy.

Born at Neuwied on the Rhine, **Adam Weisweiler** became one of the most brilliant *ébénistes* of his period. Establishing himself in Paris at the beginning of the reign of Louis XVI, he obtained his *maîtrise* in 1778 and set up shop in the rue du faubourg-Saint-Antoine where he soon distinguished himself in making very luxurious furniture. His talents brought him the patronage of the Royal Houses and especially that of the Queen, for whom he made furniture for Saint-Cloud. Provident and extending no credit for his wares, he withstood the Revolution and was able to buy a house during the Terror. His furniture, full of fantasy and imagination rivals in grace and lightness the best made by the great Riesener and Carlin. Among other of his pieces was a desk made for Marie Antoinette, probably with the co-operation of the bronze-maker Gouthière. Disappearing during the Revolution, this precious table came to light again during the reign of Napoleon III, who bought it back. It is now in the Louvre. The Wallace Collection in London has a *secrétaire* with painted porcelain plaques, busts of women at the corners and a medallion with the monogram of Marie Antoinette. Many famous museums and collections own examples by this great master, whose work was never surpassed in the Louis XVI period.

Of foreign origin, probably Scandinavian, **Pierre-Harry Mewesen** received his *maîtrise* in Paris in 1766 and lived in the rue du faubourg-Saint-Antoine for twenty years. He had great taste and was an active and very expert artist who left his signature on pieces of charming elegance.

Ferdinand Bury, 1740–1795, was made master in 1774. Besides important pieces of marquetry in mahogany and yellow woods, this cabinetmaker made many curious and original pieces such as mechanical tables, *gueridons à cremaillère, tricoteuses,* and tables with secret drawers. He employed principally German workers who had a special aptitude for this sort of work. A certain number of the bronzes he used came from the hands of Antoine-André Ravrio, a brilliant bronze worker with a reputation as great as that of Thomire. Bury deserved success because of the meticulous care he used in the fabrication of his pieces, but he entered into some unfortunate speculations, which were aggravated by the Revolution. He left some fine pieces inlaid in geometric design with exotic woods from the Indies and on one of these, acquired by Comte Isaac de Camondo which he bequeathed to the Louvre, the stamp of Riesener appears beside his own, attesting to the co-operation of these two masters.

Jacques Bircklé was one of the suppliers to the royal *Garde-Meuble* under Louis XVI. He passed his master's degree in 1764, and was known as an active and careful workman who produced numerous pieces in mahogany, *bois de rose* and marquetry for the princes and princesses of France and for the Queen at Saint-Cloud. Although he ceased to work for the Crown in 1789, his house survived the Revolution and was carried on by his son until 1825.

Louis Moreau was a notable cabinetmaker who, after passing his master's degree in September 1764, acquired the stock of his colleague Genty and continued the traditions of his predecessor. He employed such notable cabinetmakers as Bircklé, Topino, and Foullet, and the bronze-casters Guinard and Cottin, as well as the gilders Pregermain and Fagard. Under Louis XVI he received orders from the Court and is known to have made mahogany *servantes, dessertes, gueridons* and game tables of the loveliest quality, and while his stamp is on things of extremely fine taste the pieces are extremely varied. This leads to the belief that he personally did not make all of those with his name, but he was meticulous and very careful that everything bearing his signature was of outstanding quality.

Jean Charles Ellaume was given his master's degree in 1754. During his thirty years as a cabinetmaker his work was in demand and he achieved some very fine pieces of furniture, especially commodes, *secrétaires* and *bureaux plats* in the Louis XV style.

François Delorme was born in 1691 and died in 1768. Received as master in 1735, he worked in an exotic style, mostly gilded and in lacquer in the Chinese taste. When he died he left a quantity of commode carcases with the

notation that they were to be covered with lacquer. His son
Adrien who became a master in 1748 established himself
in the rue du Temple. The almanacs of the period mention him as "one of the most able and well-known *ébénistes*
for his marquetry." He continued to carry on with the
same success until 1783 when he retired and sold out at
auction, what was described as a quantity of commodes,
corner-cupboards and desks, decorated with gilded bronzes
and with marble and alabaster tops. His work shows a
pleasing and brilliant fantasy. Most of his early pieces are
in European lacquer imitating that of the East, but later
in his career he produced some fine marquetry pieces, of
which one notable example is in the Louvre. It is a tiny
worktable decorated with baskets and vases of flowers
framed in curved outlines of marquetry.

Jean-Louis Delorme, his brother, was registered as a
master in 1763. Five years later he succeeded his father
at the rue Tiquetonne and continued to run the workshop
until about 1780. **Alexis,** younger brother of the two passed
his master's examination in 1772 but soon thereafter he
abandoned cabinetmaking in favor of running a furniture
store, which disappeared in 1786.

David Roentgen was a German cabinetmaker of great
international fame. He was born near Frankfurt, Germany,
in 1743, and died in Wiesbaden in 1807. In his youth he
had begun working for his father, who was also a cabinetmaker, and he succeeded him in 1772. He formed an
association with a clockmaker named Peter Kintzing
(1746–1816) who had a fantastic talent for all mechanical
devices. These, Roentgen incorporated into his furniture,
for which he used a special process which gave wood the
appearance of marble, so hard and high was the polish.
He also invented a special treatment of marquetry which
enabled him to depict scenes and reproduce pictures with
the utmost precision.

In 1774 he embarked on his first trip to France, where
he became associated with some of his countrymen already
established in Paris and found encouragement from the
Queen, Marie Antoinette, who was always kindly disposed
to those from across the Rhine. On his second trip in 1779
he was accompanied by Kintzing and it was recorded that
"the Germans" brought a carload of precious pieces of

their work. Louis XVI, who delighted in all things mechanical, acquired a tremendous desk, eleven-feet high by five-feet wide. Its shape was like that of a building with pilasters and a façade symbolizing the liberal arts. The interior was a masterpiece of machinery, with secret drawers, springs and movable parts. The Queen acquired several fine pieces for herself and a *bureau à cylindre* decorated with Chinese subjects which she sent to Pope Pius VI as a gift. Roentgen took advantage of the publicity that his work brought him and opened a deposit of his things with a dealer named Brébant. But the cabinetmakers of the capital resented the intrusion of a foreigner and despite his protection in high places, tried to prevent him from continuing this commercial enterprise. Whereupon Roentgen sought and obtained admission to the Parisian Guild and was received as a master in 1780. He opened a shop, which he announced in the press, but he himself did not remain in Paris, only returning from time to time to keep in touch with his clients. He entrusted the sale of his merchandise to his compatriot and fellow cabinetmaker, J. G. Frost, who organized a sort of branch of the Neuwied workshop. He founded similar branches in Berlin and Vienna, made a number of trips through Germany, visited Italy, and went to Brussels to deliver two large marquetry pictures to Prince Charles of Lorraine, Governor of the Low Countries. Early in the year 1783 he lived in Russia for several months where he sold Catherine II a quantity of his furniture, which is still in the Russian museums today. Catherine was so pleased with his work that she paid more than he had asked for it and presented him with a gold snuffbox as well.

At this time, Roentgen reached the peak of his career, employing one-hundred cabinetmakers and marquetry specialists, a dozen workers in bronze, a dozen locksmiths and mechanics and several clockmakers under the direction of Kintzing. Having acquired a sizable fortune, he was also called the most celebrated cabinetmaker in Europe, by the engraver Wille, in his diary in 1787. He found a new protector in the person of Frederick-Wilhelm II, and was named official furnisher to the Court of Prussia and various other honorific titles. Unfortunately the Revolution delivered a fatal blow to his enterprise. The business that Frost had built up and of which Roentgen was the owner, went bankrupt and everything he owned in France was confiscated as the property of an alien. Then when the war became menacing and the Republican armies pillaged his workshop, Roentgen had to flee his home in Neuwied. He took refuge first in Berlin, then in Gotha and did not return to live in Neuwied until 1802. He died at the age of sixty-four during a journey to Wiesbaden. He had three sons, none of whom followed in his footsteps. Roentgen rarely signed his work except perhaps as a member of the Parisian corporation. Some pieces are marked with his initials; a few with his Christian name, David, by which he was known in France. His work, however, is easily recognizable. While the cabinetwork itself is perfection, Roentgen's furniture remains Germanic in conception and design. It is very heavy, dry and pedantic and is completely lacking in lightness and charm. His work, which was so highly prized during his lifetime is equally appreciated today.

Guillaume Beneman (or Benneman) was the principal furnisher to the Court of France during the last years of the reign of Louis XVI. Of German origin he left his country fairly late in life, with his technique and style as a cabinetmaker completely formed. Because of his German nationality which was always a recommendation to the Queen, he was commissioned in 1784 to furnish some pieces that were intended for use in the royal houses. Just at this point Riesener had fallen from grace because of his unwillingness to accommodate himself to the economic reforms instituted by the administration of the Garde-Meuble. Beneman, more modest in his pretensions and more pliable a character, inherited the honors heretofore bestowed on his famous compatriot. In August of the year 1785, a lieutenant of police addressing the community of cabinetmakers, advised them to receive Beneman into the guild with all the rights and privileges connected therewith.

Accordingly, on September 3 he was accepted as a master and the *Garde-Meuble* allocated fifteen hundred and twenty-seven livres to procure the equipment required for the use of his sixteen workmen. In the course of the next few years Beneman was engaged by the sculptor Jean Hauré who had assumed a sort of general enterprise sup-

plying furniture for the Crown, to make a great number
of pieces under his direction.

Along with many ordinary things, Beneman made some
very rich pieces with the co-operation of the modelers
Boizot, Martin and Michaud as well as from the bronze-
makers Thomire, Forestier, Bardin, and Bauchery, and
the gilders Galles and Feuchère. The first of these pieces
made for the appartements of Louis XVI at Compiègne,
were a *secrétaire* and a commode in a mosaic of colored
woods. Soon thereafter with the collaboration of the
marquetry specialist Kemp, he made a magnificent desk
which was to match the famous *secrétaire à cylindre* made
for Louis XV by Oeben and Riesener, for Versailles. Then
he delivered a commode to the Count de Provence, decorated with his monogram. For the Dauphin he made a table
in yellow wood from Guadeloupe, with bronzes by Ravrio.
Escaping from the clutches of the dominating Hauré, he
moved out of the faubourg Saint-Antoine, into the little
rue du Forez where he began work on some sumptuous
pieces for the Queen at Saint-Cloud. The Louvre has
gathered some of Beneman's principal works executed between 1787 and 1790, amongst which are two commodes
with the monogram of Marie Antoinette and large garlands
of flowers, another with the attributes of love, and two with
Sèvres plaques. After a design by Lalonde and of a more
masculine character, he made a commode for the bedchamber of the King at Saint-Cloud with the collaboration
of his colleague Stockel. Two lacquer commodes are also
mentioned, having emblems of war in bronze, which were
made by Thomire and Forestier after wax models by the
sculptor Jerome-François Marlin.

Beneman, having the title of "Cabinetmaker to the
King," continued to work for the Court until the fall of
the monarchy. During the Terror the *Garde-Meuble* ordered some modest pieces of furniture for the use of the
officials at the *Concièrgerie*. Beneman was also kept busy
eliminating coats of arms, crowns and other emblems of
nobility from the furniture confiscated from the escaped
nobles. During the Directoire his workshop became con-
structively active again. There followed a lawsuit between
Beneman and his former collaborator Thomire, who had
owed the master money since 1790. Thomire suggested,

vainly, paying it off in work, but Beneman would not accept these terms and the only concession Thomire was able to achieve was extension of a period of grace in which to pay.

The Château of Fontainebleau has two precious pieces by Beneman produced at the beginning of the Consulate period which were made after a design by Percier for Bonaparte. Beneman's career seems to have ended soon thereafter. His work is remarkable for the beauty of the materials and the delicacy and finesse of the work rather than for the design. His works show a German rather than a French taste, his pieces are heavy, and their proportions leave something to be desired.

Guillaume Kemp, a native of Germany, worked on the faubourg Saint-Antoine in 1757 when he married the daughter of the master cabinetmaker **Péridiez.** After acquiring his own master's degree in 1764, he continued working until the Revolution. He is known for his extraordinarily fine and meticulous work, collaborating with his colleague Beneman in 1786 on the construction of a grandiose desk for Louis XV at the Palais de Versailles. Kemp executed the marquetry fruits and flowers after a cartoon by the painter Gerard Van Spaendonck. His exquisite pieces have been much sought after and are to be found in some of the great collections.

Joseph Gegenbach known as **Canabas,** a notable cabinetmaker was born around 1715 and died in 1797. He was the son of an artisan, probably of Alsatian origin. Canabas came to Paris early in life and in 1745 married Marie Parmentier, the daughter of a colleague. His talents were recognized and employed by the great dealers of the period such as Pierre Migeon and Jean-François Oeben, to whom he sold a variety of the odd pieces of furniture in which he specialized. He became a master in 1766. At the death of his wife, three years later, an inventory of his stock showed a large number of little tables, *servantes, guéridons* and screens. His business grew to such proportions that he was obliged to move to larger quarters. Despite the great difficulties, he was able to save his business from ruin and to keep it going during the Revolution, but he succumbed under the Directoire.

At his death his merchandise was sold at public auction

and was composed of *secrétaires,* commodes, bureaus, *guéridons,* tables of many kinds, consoles, toilet tables for both sexes, *chiffonières, fauteuils de bureaux,* and other items, almost all of which were made in solid mahogany, decorated with brasses in the latest taste of the time. His pieces are often original in form and always of beautiful workmanship.

Jean-François Dubut, a cabinetmaker of excellent reputation even during his lifetime, died in 1778. His merchandise was dispersed at public auction and consisted of bookcases, *secrétaires* with cupboards, flat-top desks, *bureaux à cylindre,* tables, and all kinds of corner-cupboards, *chiffonières,* dressing tables, etc., all of which were in mahogany. He treated *bois des Indes* with great skill and his work is represented in some fine collections.

Joseph Schmitz was a little known but highly skillful cabinetmaker who despite his German name was not a German. He was born in Paris, passed his master's degree in 1761, and produced furniture which shows the greatest care and meticulous workmanship. Most of his furniture is in the Louis XV style but some pieces of Louis XVI are also known to exist and all are of charming shape and some with extraordinary flower marquetry.

CHAPTER FIFTEEN

Menuisiers

Among the greatest *menuisiers* or workers in solid wood in the Louis XV period were various members of the family of **Charles Cressent**, the *ébéniste*. These included **Jacques-Louis, Jean-Baptiste, Louis, Michel, René** and perhaps others whose names and identity are not clear. All of these men spelled their name **Cresson.**

Jean Baptiste Tilliard, 1685–1766, was a member of a family of furniture makers of unusual ability and a master of the noble *bergère* and *fauteuil*. His carving is crisp, deep-cut and very sharp, usually showing a heart-shaped device in the center of each back and apron of his chairs. The lines are flowing and graceful but despite the intricately carved flowers and crestlike device they retain a strong masculine quality. Father and son worked for the Crown throughout their lives and their magnificent work is represented in most great museums and in the world's finest collections. The son, Jacques-Jean-Baptiste or **Jean Baptiste the Second,** carried on his father's traditions brilliantly. The signature of Tilliard was used successively in the same form by father and son, so it may be concluded that the pieces of an earlier date can be attributed to the father and those of later date to the son, who lived until 1797. The best of their work was done between 1740 and 1760.

Nicolas-Quimbert Foliot furnished a great many beds, screens, *canapés* (sofas) and stools for Versailles, Trianon, Compiègne, Fontainebleau and Saint-Aubert. He also made the magnificent base for Louis XV's throne at Versailles and a whole set of furniture for the King's bedroom, which was bequeathed to the Musée du Louvre by the late Count Isaac de Camondo. An exquisite bed made for Marie Antoinette while she was still the dauphine added to his glories. He was the son of Nicolas Foliot who had been the official *menuisier* of the Royal Household from 1723 until his death in 1749, when Nicolas-Quimbert took over. François, his younger brother, who was also a sculptor was known as **Foliot le Jeune.** He, in turn, left a very able son, **Toussaint-François** who carried on the family tradition upon the death of his father and later that of his mother, who had conducted the workshop during her son's boyhood. After producing some extraordinary pieces for Louis XVI, such as the bed in the winter bedroom of the King, another in chinoiserie style for the bedroom of Marie Antoinette at Oisy and numerous masterpieces for the Court and the Academy of Sciences at the Louvre, he retired in 1786. His pieces were mostly unmarked except for those stamped with his father's mark, F. Foliot.

François Reuze (1716–99) was the son of a *menuisier,* Pierre Reuze, and became a master in 1743. He produced chairs of most exceptional quality and received orders from the Swedish Crown as well as from Marie Antoinette for the Petit Trianon. His work during the Louis XV period showed great originality of ornamentation, featuring rocaille forms, especially on the insides of chair frames. His furniture is of exquisite quality.

Jean-Jacques Pothier was received as a master in 1750. He worked until 1780 making chairs, *canapés,* and similar furniture, which is distinguished by the beautiful shape of the frames and the graceful details. His signature is found on a set belonging to the *Mobilier National* and on another which he made for Malmaison toward the end of his career.

Père Gourdin or Jean Gourdin was the first of that name to produce very fine chairs and *canapés.* He flourished between 1737 and 1763 and is the author of furniture of extraordinary quality and beauty. A number of his pieces form a part of the Royal Collection of Sweden. His son, **Jean-Baptiste Gourdin,** was received as a master in 1748 and established himself near his father. His talents were employed by the Prince de Soubise and he worked until 1776. His chairs, like those of his father, were noble in character and have found their way into great collections.

Michel Gourdin, called Gourdin le Jeune, a brother of Jean-Baptiste acquired his *maîtrise* in 1752 and is the author of some splendid chairs in the finest Louis XV style and of superb quality.

Nicolas Heurtaut, a notable French *menuisier* in the Louis XV period, was the son of an artisan of the same profession and probably the nephew of his namesake Nicolas Heurtaut, the sculptor and member of the Academy of Saint-Luc. Born in 1720, he passed his master's examination in 1755 and established himself in a shop in which he enjoyed great success for twenty years, producing beds, chairs, *canapés*, etc. His work is of excellent quality and has long been collected by the knowledgeable and the fastidious.

Blanchard is the surname of a family of Parisian *menuisiers*. The first known, **Nicolas Blanchard,** became a master in 1738 and resided in the rue de Cléry. He was still in business in 1749 when he took part in a counter-lawsuit against the chair workers who had formed a union in order to force their employers to pay higher salaries. He left his signature on chairs in walnut with rocaille forms.

Sylvain-Nicolas, oldest son of the preceding, was born in 1725, obtained his master's degree at the age of eighteen in 1743 and opened a shop in the same street as his father. In 1758 he was elected arbiter by the judge-consuls in litigation between his colleague Annest and a furniture dealer. He apparently died before the end of the Louis XV reign. Pieces signed by him are of very graceful design, but rare.

Jean-Nicolas called **le Jeune,** brother of Sylvain Nicolas, was born around 1730 and was received as a master in 1771, after the death of his brother whose shop he took over. He became official furniture maker to the Royal family, to whom he delivered some magnificent pieces decorated with roses, cupids and garlands of flowers. An imposing set was made for the Aunts of the King at the Château de Bellevue.

Jean Boucault, Parisian chair-maker was born around 1705 and died in 1786. Having earned his master's degree in 1728, he established himself in the rue de Cléry where he carried on for years. He is responsible for work of excellent design. Two of his chairs are in the Musée Carnavalet, and other fine pieces have passed through the auction rooms. He retired after more than fifty years of conscientious application to his art.

Avisse is the name of a Parisian family which distinguished itself in making beds and chairs of high quality. **Michel Avisse** delivered chairs to the *Garde Meuble* in 1740 and he is known to have made chairs with caned seats and backs. **Guillaume Avisse,** son of the preceding, was born in 1720 and matured in his father's workshop. When in 1743 he became a master he opened an atelier of his own. Under Louis XVI he moved to the rue du Faubourg-Saint-Denis, but his workshop disappeared between 1782 and 1785.

Jean Avisse, born in 1723, acquired his master's degree in 1745. Eighteen months later he established himself in the rue de Cléry, assisted in his business by his wife Marie-Anne Gourdin who was a member of the family of famous *menuisiers* of that name. The quality of his work and the moderate prices attracted hordes of furniture dealers as well as private clients and the nobility. Despite his great popularity, he went through a period of financial embarrassment, with which he was happily able to cope without serious consequences. He continued to work at the same address until the Revolution, when he was seventy-three years old. He is known principally for his fine Louis XV chairs, remarkable for the nobility of their design and their sober elegance. Some, however, are very richly carved, and he is represented by a chair with tiny flowers in the Musée des Arts Décoratifs and by a *bergère* which forms a part of the collection of the *Mobilier National,* as well as in various great private collections. There was also a superb *canapé* with *rocailles* and garlands in the old collection of the late Paul Dutasta.

Jean-Baptiste Boulard, Parisian *menuisier,* was one of the official furnishers to the Crown. He was born around

1725 and died in 1789. After passing his master's degree, in 1754, he established himself in the rue de Cléry and soon acquired a reputation which made him eligible for the honor of being attached to the service of the *Garde-Meuble*. Thereafter he executed a considerable number of pieces, the most important of which was the magnificent and elaborate bed for Louis XVI at Fontainebleau.

Another of his principal achievements was a set comprising twelve pieces of very rich furniture for the study of the King at Saint-Cloud. He also supplied a huge conference table for the King, and a table for the Queen at Versailles, and also a bed in which Gustave III of Sweden slept during his visit to Versailles, as well as a cradle for Princess Sophie, born in 1786. He delivered chairs for the apartments of Madame Louise and Madame Elizabeth and also the Count and Countess de Provence. The Comte d'Artois had him compete for the installation of the "Château de Bagatelle" and expressly requested eight large *bergères* with a matching screen carved by the sculptor J. B. Rode. Boulard was often honored by being asked to mediate in professional trade disputes and became chief deputy for his corporation. After his death, his widow carried on and continued to supply the Royal Household until the fall of the monarchy. Later his descendants worked again for the Imperial Palaces of Napoleon, but the workshop in the rue de Cléry disappeared in 1823.

J. B. Boulard signed with two different signatures; one of these is found only on pieces of the pure Louis XV style; the other on things of the Louis XVI period, of which there are many more. His chairs are characterized by the generosity of their proportions, which were very uncommon at that time. The Mobilier National has a number of examples, one of which is on exhibition at the Louvre. The Elysée Palace and the Ministry of the Interior also have some admirable chairs by this master. In the old Jacques Doucet Collection there was a pair of splendid stools originally from the *Château de Compiègne*. Other famous private collections include pieces of unusual merit.

Louis-Charles Carpentier obtained his master's degree in 1752 and worked during the reign of Louis XV. He made chairs of beautiful line and character, examples of which are on display at the Musée des Arts Décoratifs in Paris, the Musée des Arts Décoratifs in Strasbourg, the Musée Jacquemart-André in Paris and were owned before their dispersal and sale by some of France's most distinguished and knowledgeable nineteenth-century collectors.

Pierre Bara who acquired his master's degree in 1758, and his cousin **Charles Vincent Bara** were both *menuisiers* of standing during the Louis XV period. Their signatures are sometimes found on chairs of excellent quality.

Pierre Remy was born in Paris in 1724 and died in August 1798. The son of a cabinetmaker and a descendant of the famous Gilles Joubert, he became an outstanding *menuisier* whose work is distinguished by the noble elegance of design apparent in the simpler as well as the more elaborate examples of his work. There is a set of signed chairs, the backs of which form a sort of crown in the *Bibliothèque de l'Arsenal,* which were originally made for the Marquis de Paulmy, Governor of the Arsenal, near the end of the reign of Louis XV. Other examples of his work are in well-known French collections.

Louis Delanois, famous Parisian cabinetmaker, was born in 1731 and died in 1792. In his youth he was employed by the widow J. B. Lerouge; he passed his *maître* on July 27, 1761, and opened a little workshop in the rue Bourbon-Villeneuve. The originality, elegance and finesse of his work attracted the great dealers of his time as well as many members of the aristocracy, such as the Prince de Beauvau and the Comte d'Orsay. Delanois also engaged in the wood industry which helped him further his cabinet work. His unusual ability gained him the protection of Mme. du Barry who commissioned him to furnish her lodgings at the Château de Fontainebleau. The sculptor Guichard and the gilder Cagny were also attached to her service. The chairs of her bedroom at Versailles were designed with finely carved roses, and she ordered an especially large armchair made for the King's use when he visited her. The list of Delanois' noble patrons is a very long one and also included the Queen. He was tremendously successful and grew rich, but was ruined by the Revolution and declared bankrupt in 1790. He died less than two years thereafter.

Philippe-Joseph Pluvinet was received as a master on July 14, 1754 and continued to work until his death in

1793. He distinguished himself in the manufacture of very luxurious chairs of the Louis XVI style, of noble character and brilliant execution. He was the father of **Louis-Magdeleine Pluvinet**, also a chair-maker, but of lesser stature.

Claude Chevigny, who became a master *menuisier* in 1768, distinguished himself in the manufacture of deluxe chairs and other seat furniture. He made a set for the Duc de Choiseuil at Chanteloup which now decorates the Chamber of Commerce building at Tours. The *Mobilier National* owns several examples of this master's work, including some that were originally made for the Palais de Fontainebleau.

Jean Baptiste Bernard Demay was a Parisian *menuisier* who gained his master's degree in 1784 and worked with great success for thirty years. At the beginning of his career he received orders for whole sets of furniture for the Queen, among which are some chairs with Marie Antoinette's monogram, now at the Petit Trianon. At the Musée Carnavalet there are chairs à *la Montgolfière* suggestive of the balloon ascension which captured the imagination of the public at that time. After the Revolution, Demay used a different signature which included his address, and his workshop finally disappeared at the end of the Empire period during the depression which ruined all French industry.

The celebrated **Jacob family** were workers in hard wood for almost a century. The first and greatest of them all was **Georges Jacob,** who was born in Cheny in Burgundy in 1739 and died in Paris in 1814. Around the age of sixteen he came to the capital to learn the art of working in wood and started with decorative sculpture, supposedly in the establishment of Louis Delanois, where he developed the delicacy of his taste and his creative genius. On September 4, 1765 Jacob won his master's degree, submitting as his *chef-d'oeuvre* a small model of an armchair which his descendants still possess. He abandoned his first workshop for a larger place in the rue Meslay, and from 1773 on he received orders from the *Garde-Meuble Royal*. He was given several tasks such as the repair of some Boulle furniture, but his tastes ran to chairs, beds, screens, consoles, and *torchères,* which he not only designed, but carried out entirely himself, including the carving. In that specialty he surpassed all of his rivals in the perfection of his technique. His brilliant fantasy gave even his more modest pieces nobility, grace and a certain distinction. His fertile imagination created new forms of harmonious elegance. Chairs with round seats, console feet, and lyre backs were among his innovations and he was the first to use mahogany for chairs. His brilliant inventiveness brought him the favor of Marie Antoinette who loved novelty and before she became Queen he executed many pieces in the allegorical taste of the period. The most extraordinary, however, were made for the boudoir at Versailles after she was Queen. These chairs included in their design such emblems as torches, quivers, attributes of love, sphinxes, and symbols of mystery, and fidelity, as well as cocks' and eagles' heads, and the emblems of France and Austria.

Many of these pieces are in the Kunstgewerbe Museum in Berlin, while the Musée des Arts Décoratifs in Paris possesses three other fine chairs, the feet of which are in the form of quivers, the arms in the shape of horns of plenty and the backs decorated with the Austrian eagle surmounted with roses. These latter pieces were created for the bedroom of the Queen at Saint-Cloud.

The list of Jacob's great patrons and the pieces he made for them is too long to enumerate. However, an interesting development must be mentioned. The painter David, who copied his models from the drawings on Etruscan vases, wanted to own a set of furniture closely resembling that of the Greeks and Romans of antiquity and entrusted this task to Georges Jacob. The chairs were fashioned of the darkest mahogany in order to resemble the patina of old bronze and it was in this manner that the Empire style was born.

The friendship between David and Jacob led to a close co-operation in launching the new style. Later when David's republican enthusiasm reached its climax he arranged to have Jacob commissioned to supply the new conference room in the Palais des Tuileries. David himself designed a chair draped in purple for the presidential seat. The stalls for seven-hundred-and-sixty deputies, benches for the public, desks for the secretaries and the great tribunal supported by two griffins were designed by the architects Percier and Fontaine, still young beginners freshly returned from their studies in Rome. Within several months Georges Jacob was able to carry out this tremendous project.

During the Terror the painter Simon Julien painted Jacob's portrait in a tricolor costume—blue suit, red vest and a white cravat—an obvious suggestion of his sympathy for the new order, dictated by caution rather than conviction. Being rich, he was suspect and on several occasions envious people denounced him to the Committee of Public Safety. Protected as he was by his friend David, who had a seat in that sinister council, Jacob was apparently neither arrested nor imprisoned despite the rumors. During the Directoire period Jacob vigorously applied himself to the manufacture of furniture of all kind; and under the difficulties that existed he made less elaborate furniture in mahogany, maple or lemonwood with incrustations of ebony and amaranth. This was certainly not the sort of furniture on which he had built his great reputation and his fortune.

In the spring of 1796 Georges Jacob handed over the direction of his business to his two sons, Georges and François-Honoré who were registered under the new order as **Jacob Frères.** Both had been born in Paris, the older in 1768, the younger in 1770. In their joint enterprise under the Consulate, the older was the administrator while the younger was the technician and called himself Jacob-Desmalter, taking the name of a small estate owned by his father in Burgundy. Extremely intelligent, he loved his profession and was so gifted that contemporaries considered his work comparable to that of Boulle in the seventeenth century and of Riesener in the eighteenth. Luck was with the brothers from the start for General Bonaparte, returning from Italy, commissioned them to make a curious set of furniture for his bedroom at the rue Chantereine in which the bed resembled a tent and the chairs were in the form of drums. Later he ordered the Jacob Frères to refurnish the royal residences which had been devastated by the Revolution. Up to that point, having made very sober pieces, the main virtue of which was the purity of line, the Jacob Frères began making much richer furniture decorated with sculpture and bronzes. Sometimes there were insets of colored woods or porcelain plaques imitating

Wedgwood. They received a prize at an exposition for two commodes decorated with cameos. Included among the furniture they submitted were three-footed tripod incense burners, and a sumptuous carved and gilded console topped by an Italian mosaic. They now signed with a new stamp which included the name of their street. Many of these pieces still exist and are the property of the state.

The older brother died very young, so François-Honoré formed a new association with his father under the name of **Jacob Desmalter & Cie.** When he became the official cabinetmaker to the Emperor his business developed prodigiously and he had at least fifteen workshops, of which seven were devoted to cabinetmaking, both furniture and chairs; three to carving, painting and gilding of wood, three to bronze, one to tapestry, and one to mechanical locks. He produced a vast amount of furniture which Napoleon wished to use in the restoration of all the palaces now in his estates. The Imperial Throne at Fontainebleau, the jewel cabinet of Marie Louise, the buffets in ebony for Versailles and the grandiose sets of chairs which Jacob made, chiefly on designs by Percier and Fontaine with the co-operation of the bronze-makers Thomire and Ravrio, give one an idea of the huge number of things he produced. He also furnished the courts of Holland, Spain, Russia, and Westphalia. At the end of the Empire when this vast establishment was ruined, as were all the others, by the crisis which paralyzed the entire national industry, Jacob retired. But his son **Georges-Alphonse Jacob-Desmalter,** who was born in 1799, continued the family tradition and worked for the Crown during the second part of the Restoration. An able designer, a pupil of Percier, Jacob created some good compositions, but unfortunately the taste and economic conditions of the time prevented him from continuing. In 1847 rather than debase his art he gave up the workshop and devoted the rest of his life to architecture and drawing.

Henri Jacob, a very able cabinetmaker from 1779 on, was no relative of the family of Georges Jacob. However, the similarity of the name served to advance his interests and he did not hesitate to take advantage of it. His work closely resembles that of Georges, which he imitated with such virtuosity that he earned himself a deservedly brilliant reputation. He obtained orders for the Court, and among other notable pieces for the Queen there were carved and gilded chairs and mahogany chairs of the most beautiful quality. After 1789 he added a stock of fine tables, book-cases, and *secrétaires*, but his establishment disappeared at the beginning of the Empire period. His work is on display at the Musée des Arts Décoratifs in Paris and in Strasbourg, also in Berlin and other foreign cities and collections.

The famous name **Sené** was that of a family of Parisian *menuisiers*, the first of whom was **Jean**, born presumably around 1695. He only began signing his chairs toward the end of his period of activity, when a stamp became obligatory. He is known to have made some richly sculp-tured Régence and Louis XV pieces with *rocaille* decora-tions, *cartouches* and foliage, and to have signed his caned chairs with the signature he adopted, *Sené Lepere*.

Claude I, son of Jean, was born in 1724 and acquired his master's degree in July 1742. Having married a sister of Jean Étienne Saint-Georges, he established himself with his brother-in-law at the rue de Cléry, but although they shared the workshop each master maintained his inde-pendence and signed his own work. They remained to-gether until 1780 when Claude Sené retired and went to end his days with his oldest son, in whose house he died in 1792. His products bear the stamp with his initial *C*, closely resembling a G. He left very fine work including a splendid chair in the Louis XV style now at the Musée des Arts Décoratifs, two painted walnut chairs in the Palace of Archives, a *bergère* belonging to the Mobilier National and others in famous private collections.

Jean-Baptiste Sené, his oldest son, was born in 1748. He also acquired his degree when he was very young, in 1769, and six months thereafter established himself in rue de Cléry. An artisan of great ability and extremely industrious he acquired a brilliant reputation in his profession. From 1785 on he became *fournisseur à la Couronne* or furnisher to the Crown. The archives record descriptions of a quantity of his products including beds, chairs of all types, tables, consoles, screens, fire screens, and even dogs' beds disguised in different forms. With the co-operation of the sculptors Guérin, Alexandre and Vallois, he produced

magnificent pieces for the Château de Saint-Cloud. Those
to be used in the King's apartments presented emblems of
Force, Wisdom, Justice and Temperance; those for the
Queen displayed attributes of Love, the Lilies of France
and the Austrian eagle. For the same château he delivered
some special chairs with flexible frames which were trans-
formable into stools. For the theatre at Versailles he devised special chairs which turned. Among the more
remarkable pieces he delivered were two huge consoles
which, when joined together formed a fourteen-foot-long
table which was used as a conference table for the *Conseil
d'état,* or State Conferences. Other remarkable pieces, too
numerous to mention, were made by this great master for
the nobility of France until the fall of the monarchy. He
managed to remain in favor even thereafter, and was commissioned to make desks for the officials of the Republic.
He continued to work with great success until his death
in 1803.

His mark, J. B. Sené, is found on works of superb
quality, in no respect inferior to that of Georges Jacob.
Their elegance and finesse of execution were comparable
to the best ever produced. A good number of his pieces are
to be seen in the Palais de Compiègne, at Fontainebleau,
Trianon, and the small apartments of the Queen at Versailles. The storerooms of the *Garde-Meuble* contain other
chairs of this master, as well as the Louvre, the Musée
Condée at Chantilly, and many others.

Claude II called **le Jeune,** brother of the preceding, devoted himself to the same type of work. Admitted to the
guild as master in 1769, he took an atelier of his own on
the rue du faubourg-Saint-Denis. He soon moved to the
rue de Cléry 137, near his brother, Jean-Baptiste, and
then received some orders for the royal palaces on which
he collaborated with the sculptors Ambroise, Vinceneaux,
Cherin and Bernier. He made many folding, and other
stools for the Court, and for use in the King's room at
Compiègne. Unhappily, his workshop was extinguished by
the torments of the Revolution. Despite the same initials
as his father, his signature is easily distinguishable from
the latter's and is to be found on very good pieces of the
Louis XVI period.

Jean-Baptiste Lebas was born in 1729 and died in 1795.

Son of an artisan, he obtained his master's degree in 1756 and exercised his profession with singular ability for twenty years. Mme. du Barry recognized his talents and had him compete for the installation of the *pavilion de Louveciennes*. He furnished the Comte d'Artois with a magnificent drawing room set composed of two sofas and sixteen armchairs, whose oval backs were richly carved and showed unique fantasy and originality of design. Later this set was purchased by the Duc de Talleyrand for the Château de Valency where it was used by the King of Spain, Ferdinand VII during his captivity in France. The salon of the King in the Grand Trianon was composed of one *canapé* and six *fauteuils* by Lebas, remarkable for their great elegance of design and execution. Others of his finely carved pieces are in the style of Delafosse. The Mobilier National, the Musée des Arts Décoratifs and the Royal Swedish Collection possess examples of this master. Jean-Baptiste Lebas signed his work J. Lebas. His two sons and pupils, who continued to work after the father's retirement until the end of the eighteenth century, used the name Lebas, omitting the *J* of the father's signature.

Sulpice Brizard, a Paris *menuisier* was born around 1735 and died after 1798. Having married Marie-Geneviève Meunier, the daughter of an artisan in his field, he acquired his master's degree in 1763 according to the conditions accorded sons-in-law of established masters. Three years later he opened his own workshop where he produced chairs of exceptional quality. He is reputed to have been one of the chief furnishers of seat furniture to the Court during the early years of the reign of Louis XVI. His chairs were of remarkably fine quality and some of them are in the Garde-Meuble National. He is also represented in the Musée du Louvre by a set of four chairs from the Comando Collection. The Metropolitan Museum of Art in New York has a fine oval-backed gilded *canapé* signed by this master, made in co-operation with the cabinetmaker Louis Delanois who furnished the rest of the same set.

His brother Pierre Brizard followed the same profession but did not achieve a reputation such as that enjoyed by Sulpice.

PART FIVE

CHAPTER SIXTEEN

Advice to Collectors

Collecting antiques is one of the most absorbing hobbies and one that can be continued into old age. As people advance in years and spend more hours at home, it is a great joy to be surrounded by lovely things of the past and whether one collects items of great or of minor monetary value, the thrill of a discovery or of filling a gap in one's collection is an exhilarating experience. Much has already been written on French art and it continues to be explored. An eager student will find a great deal of information to be gleaned if he has the patience to wade through some of the more technical books on the subject.

There are fashions in art as in other fields for what the public wants at a given time may leave a subsequent generation completely cold. This does not mean that the public's taste has improved. It is only a temporary change. In time, the pendulum swings the other way again and some neglected period is rediscovered and appreciated by those who are weary of what they see about them. A contributing factor to the public's tiring of a style of decoration is a reaction against the constant repetition of the use of the same colors, fabrics and specific pieces of furniture by everyone trying to decorate a room in a given style. After seeing the decoration of the house of some fashionable person, others attempt to make their own resemble it as closely as possible.

During the first three decades of the twentieth century Gothic and Renaissance decorations were the great vogue. Important collections such as that of the Davanzati Palace in Florence, the Bardini, Volpi and the Tolentino collections were sold in New York at public auction and collectors paid huge prices for the fifteenth-and-sixteenth-century pieces that were offered. One was considered fortunate to possess pieces from these great collections in which the pieces were authentic and of rare quality. In 1930 the famous Figdor Collection was sold in Vienna and aroused such interest that people from all corners of the globe attended the sale. Such pieces being scarce and correspondingly expensive, as well as requiring large, high-ceilinged rooms to set off their beauty, were beyond the reach of the general public. Many could not or did not wish to live in what they considered a museum atmosphere and veered to English furniture which they found less formal. Simultaneously with the vogue for French Gothic and Italian Renaissance, there was a great interest in Jacobean oak from England.

Since there is never enough good antique furniture in existence to fill the demand, vulgar imitations are produced to give what is naïvely believed to be the same effect. Some decorators try to be gay and original with period furniture but their abortive attempts are all too frequently tawdry and ridiculous. When the market is flooded with these ugly interpretations of a given period a reaction against it is sure to follow. So it was when theatres and movie houses, restaurants and apartment house lobbies were decorated in what was believed to be the Renaissance style. Orange-tinted electric light bulbs added to the dreary vulgarity of these hideous and utterly inappropriate halls.

When a reaction set in against so-called heavy, dark and austere furniture of the French and Italian fifteenth and sixteenth centuries, and when even English seventeenth-century oak seemed depressing, the public fancy veered to Queen Anne walnut which thereupon became the great fashion. A generation later saw the children of those who had collected Queen Anne turn toward Georgian mahogany and English Regency, which were then considered very smart even in reproductions.

Many who favored French eighteenth-century interiors

throughout this time frowned upon what some call "palace furniture" as too elegant to be in keeping with the simplicity of the American way of life and wanted provincial things. During the financial depression in the United States, a great department store coined the expression: "It's smart to be thrifty." This spirit pervaded many people's thinking and thus a simple, provincial atmosphere was sought, although sometimes at a very high cost.

Oddly enough, throughout the nineteen-fifties as the lack of servants made life even more informal, very elegant French eighteenth-century furniture returned to new heights of popularity all over the world and many people would not consider any other style for their interiors.

Within the past few years, the long-neglected Renaissance and seventeenth-century furniture is slowly attracting attention. Interest in it is very wisely being revived by some young decorators who are finding new ways of using it charmingly even in ultra-modern houses and apartments. A few good, early pieces do marvels in relieving a modern interior of its blank, lifeless appearance.

The much discussed question of an article's value is a very interesting subject, but is extremely difficult to determine. True, there is a so-called market value for run-of-the-mill objects which are frequently offered, but as a piece of exceptional quality is very rarely encountered, no exact figure can be set. A very fine piece in any field retains or increases its value to a far greater extent than a mediocre one, whether it be furniture or a jewel. However, even the more ordinary antique pieces are now growing scarce and prices are rising to such an extent that estimates are often very inaccurate. Newspapers and a number of magazines report sale prices at public auction as a guide to collectors, but these are extremely misleading because they do not tell the whole story.

In most countries there are groups of dealers who form rings. There is an understanding between them that only one of their number will do the bidding and the rest do not compete at a sale. This enables them to obtain an object for a much lower figure than if each were to act independently. Immediately after the auction this group meets again and a second little auction called a "Revision" follows, at which the ultimate purchaser pays off the others in equal shares.

The man who purchased an object at the sale was acting, not for himself alone, but for whatever number of other dealers were interested in it originally. Later the dealers meet at an agreed place and hour and sit around a table while one of their number keeps the score. The first man bids a certain sum that he is willing to pay, over and above the purchase price. Let us say, for instance, that he offers the equivalent of twenty-five dollars. Going around the table each man then meets the figure of twenty-five dollars. The second time around the first man bids another twenty-five dollars and each one who meets his bid remains in the pool. When one of the number drops out, he ceases to be entitled to a share of the future bidding from that time on. His share is determined by the number of men entered in the "Revision" and the point at which he stopped bidding. If there are only four participating, he gets a quarter of whatever was bid up to the time that he dropped out. The eventual purchaser, is the one offering twenty-five dollars more than any of the others, and is also entitled to his quarter of the bids. Thus his final purchase price is whatever he has offered over-and-above the others, less his share of the money offered above the original purchase price at the auction. The fewer the participants of the "Revision" the greater the profit for those entering it. Since the number of shares depends on the number of contestants, the profit shrinks whenever there are many taking part.

It is possible for a member of the group to make a very substantial sum of money without actually buying a single item, while the highest bidder may be obliged to pay as much as double, or three times the amount for which the piece was sold at auction some hours earlier. This is why reports of auction prices mean very little, unless the item is purchased independently by a private collector.

Many people enjoy buying at auction; they feel that they are buying at the source, some erroneously believing that they get bargains at public sales and are avoiding the payment of a dealer's profit. The excitement of an auction is tremendously stimulating, with some of the elements of a horse race. The thrill of winning out over an opponent leads many to stretch a point and pay more than they had anticipated.

The previous owner's name plays a great role in stimulating interest in a collection and keen competition at a sale. The same objects offered without the glamorous name of a socially-prominent owner fetch a much lower price. Perhaps the fact that there is always an "underbidder" who is willing to pay almost as much as the purchaser himself, inspires confidence, but after the excitement of the salesroom is over, it is often difficult to recapture even the under-bidder's offer. This is frequently demonstrated when a few odd lots are purchased in error or there is some confusion concerning the bid. When offered a few weeks later, after the excitement of the sale has died down, they generally bring less money.

The question of *provenance* (or pedigree) of a piece is, of course, extremely interesting but of far less importance than is generally attached to it. Big collectors have been known to possess some poor things, even forgeries, and certainly most of them have made some errors in taste and judgment. I have heard it said with great wisdom that one must buy with one's eyes and not with one's ears. Stories connected with works of art are very intriguing and they fire the imagination, but alas, not all of them are true, and the only safe judge of merit is careful observation and examination.

At auctions many prices have soared because two or more people have fallen in love with one item which they each want at any price. Had the same piece not been exhibited at an auction gallery, which hundreds of people attend, these enthusiasts might never have troubled to look for the piece. Furthermore, they know that they must act at once or lose the object forever, whereas when seen in a gallery, innumerable vacillating characters temporize for months or years before making up their minds.

If a sale is advertised as being "unrestricted" it is against the law in America to put an "upset price" on a piece, without announcing it in advance. An "upset price" is one set by the seller below which the piece will not be sold. However, there are various methods employed by consigners to protect their things if they do not reach the minimum goal. It is therefore not always what it seems to be, if a piece is knocked down for a ridiculously low price. In all probability it simply was not sold at all. After a lapse of time the same item will re-appear, again and again, until it is finally disposed of at a reasonable figure.

There are habitués seen regularly at auctions who rarely, if ever, make a purchase. For them, it is a free spectacle and they enjoy watching others spend their money—often foolishly—according to their views, while they themselves remain aloof, enjoying a vicarious thrill. A good deal can perhaps be learned by attending sales regularly if one has a certain knowledge upon which to base observations and conclusions, or if one is keen and learns readily. But listening to the drone of the auctioneer's voice for hours and hours each week is more stultifying than educational unless one is very alert and especially interested in certain pieces.

The psychology of an auction is a curious phenomenon. When a person wishes to sell some possession, he feels certain he will obtain the highest possible price at auction. On the other hand, people who want to buy bargains attend auctions avidly because they are equally sure that they will be getting things more cheaply than in a shop! Contradictory as it may seem, both of these points of view are based on truth, but it is chance in each case which proves the deciding factor. At a sale which arouses little public interest one can, at times, buy very cheaply, but to do so one must know the merchandise.

Some are impelled to buy things at auction merely because the competition thrills them and not because they have any need or even a desire to possess such an article. They are stimulated into action through the competitive atmosphere of a sale. It would appear as though these irresponsible bidders were a boon to the auctioneers but this is not always the case. With the same spontaneity which made them buy the piece in the first place, they decide that they do not want it at all and refuse to pay for or pick it up. The auction houses try to protect themselves from such indecision by demanding a twenty-five per cent deposit immediately after a piece has been knocked down or the whole purchase price in cases where they think there is any danger of the purchaser reneging later.

At auction everything is sold "as is." In other words,

in whatever condition one may find. If there are hidden repairs in porcelains or any other serious or insignificant defects which come to light after the sale, one has no redress. This holds true for furniture as well, which sometimes collapses when it is moved to its destination. Frequently the upholstery fabric is all that holds some pieces together and once the material is removed it becomes very clear that nothing can be done without taking the piece all apart and re-doweling, re-gluing and re-upholstering it. This is an opportune moment to have strong corner blocks made for chairs and *canapés*. These are a great help in holding antique seat-furniture steady and in no way prejudices the authenticity or value of the piece.

As a rule, auction houses catalogue things to the best of their knowledge and according to what the consignors tell them, but they assume no responsibility should the attribution prove incorrect. However, if they state that an article is silver or gold for instance, then one may be certain that it is, since these materials can be tested. Items described in a catalogue as dating from a specific period are generally only in the style of that time unless the appropriate century is mentioned in the description.

In America, sales are often successfully held on the estate of a deceised owner, but even then the best pieces, if they are really important, are brought to the auction galleries in the city. The modern furnishings of a house, its carpets, curtains and other appointments look much better in the setting for which they were made than in an untidy heap at an auction house, which has no space or time to waste on showing them advantageously. In America estate sales on the premises are quite likely to be bona fide with nothing of great value offered.

In Europe antiques are frequently "planted" in private houses to which the unsuspecting are taken to see the property of a recently bereaved and needy widow, or an impoverished nobleman. If a sale results, the space formerly occupied by the commode, table or buffet which the dupe acquired will quickly be filled with another piece of suitable size to give an impression of having been there for many years.

In retail shops people almost always expect to be allowed to try furniture, pictures and art objects at home, often remarking that they wish to see if they can "live with them." If purchased at auction they seem to have no such problem and go ahead with a confidence conspicuously lacking on other occasions. When buying in Europe they do the same! A good exercise for a would-be collector is to learn to visualize things in the settings in which he hopes to place them.

There are a number of things on which to concentrate one's attention in order to detect spurious pieces although imitators have many different methods of giving false pieces the appearance of being genuine and they are diabolically clever at it.

The first step in acquiring knowledge is to read, look, touch and familiarize oneself with the history of the periods in which one is interested and the shapes and general character of the objects of that time. Practice is indispensable and one must persevere in observing details, analyzing and comparing, and turning over thousands of pieces of furniture and other objects.

It is impossible to explain how to recognize different types of wood but when, in a catalogue of an exhibition or a museum, the description mentions the wood, it should be carefully observed and memorized so that one will recognize it in the future. In the Gothic period oak was used to a large extent and was stained a dark brown. The Renaissance brought walnut into use and its lighter tones and close grain gave a somewhat less austere appearance to the furniture made with it. Ebony was a popular wood for the deluxe furniture of the seventeenth century; often incrusted with brass or ivory and accompanied by tortoise shell in various tints; sometimes inlaid with semiprecious stones. Walnut continued, nevertheless, to be the chief wood used for chairs and for simpler cabinets and tables. In the short Régence period and during the early years of the Louis XV reign some very finely carved and gilded chairs and consoles were made of oak, to match the woodwork of the period. The Louis XV period saw the use of beechwood for much of the best "seat furniture," but walnut continued to be used for chairs, especially in the provinces. For commodes, cabinets and tables veneered *bois de rose, bois de violette* and amaranth, together with other exotic woods became the favorites, while the provinces continued to use walnut and a considerable amount of *merisier* (fruitwood). In the seaport towns, mahogany from the Indies was used as early as the Louis XV period, but was only in general use in the Louis XVI period in Paris. Beechwood, either painted or gilded continued to be the preferred wood of the *menuisiers* of the Louis XVI period and mahogany, so very popular for all other furniture was rarely used for chairs until the end of the Louis XVI period, but then continued throughout the Directoire and the Empire. Oak was again used in the Louis XVI period for finely carved and gilded frames, mirrors and consoles.

The paint used on furniture in the Louis XV period was a soft blue, celadon green, grayish-white, sometimes with touches of rose or gilded outlines. The chief color of the Louis XVI reign is known as *gris Trianon,* a name given in the nineteenth century to describe what had originally been white. With the Directoire, colors grew somewhat brighter and heavier, with yellow and olive green a popular combination, or bright blue with gray. Most Empire casefurniture was made of mahogany, but painted pieces were of other woods and followed the general color schemes of their silks; a strong green or red ground with the pattern carried out in a gold color. *Citronnier* (lemonwood) which had been introduced in the Louis XVI period became the wood in highest favor during the Restoration and the reign of Charles X.

Very obvious imitations in the realm of furniture are those in which the wood has been "distressed" through artificial means, such as hitting it with heavy chains, hammer blows, etc. Old rusty tacks are apparently left in chairs and rows of nail holes with bits of old fabric still attached are made to suggest much previous upholstery. Completely spurious pieces are the easiest to detect. Much more difficult to recognize are those which were made years ago, with more care. There are meticulously made copies of eighteenth-century models which date from the second half of the nineteenth century with no intentional attempt to mislead. Somehow they make an unsatisfactory impression on a trained eye, however, for details were frequently exaggerated and over-accentuated.

People often complain that French furniture is too fancy. Genuine pieces of the eighteenth century are not fancy but copyists carve as many roses, shells and other decorative devices as the piece will hold in order to produce an effect of richness. At first glance such a piece should be suspect.

Care must be used in buying painted furniture as paint is frequently an expedient to hide the new wood under it, but not all painted furniture is doubtful. The patina of time which is beautiful to a trained eye, is not always appreciated and sometimes considered synonymous with dirt. Genuine patina is a valuable adjunct which should be appreciated and respected. Original paint of the period is a rare joy to a collector, for if the paint is of the eighteenth century the piece it covers must necessarily be genuine.

Veneered furniture frequently gives itself away if it is modern as the color is too pale and too raw and sometimes too pink or too yellow to be of the eighteenth century. Nor has it the depth of color that it should have. Copies, no matter how cleverly made, never achieve the warm golden tone that sings. Antique veneer is uneven in thickness whereas new veneer which is cut by machine, is always of uniform depth.

If, by looking at a piece, one is in doubt as to its age, it is well to touch and feel it. The sense of touch is, at times, very revealing, especially in furniture with carving. If genuinely antique, it will have been rounded and softened by time, and never have sharp edges. Old furniture has been dusted, rubbed, cleaned and waxed for something like two centuries and is soft and smooth to the touch. Clever fakers know this and try to file down corners, brush vigorously with a wire brush and do what they can to produce the effect of usage, but their efforts are never completely successful and fool only the inexperienced. Knowing this, fakers often paint the pieces in question so the telltale signs will be obliterated.

With veneered furniture the sense of touch is equally useful, as antique veneer has waves, unevennesses and other defects due to its age and reactions to climate and temperature.

Having looked and touched the piece in question one can resort to a further test. Old wood from which all the sap has been dried through the years is heavy; new wood is lighter. Of course, there is the problem of upholstery which can be responsible for extreme weight. In that case a piece must be stripped down to the frame to gauge its weight. But if the object in question is a chair, this may be unnecessary for in turning it over one can generally be certain by looking at its underside. If not covered by paint or a preparation for gilding, the underside of a beechwood piece is of a rosy, warm, light-brown color which no one has ever succeeded in imitating and which, through practice, one learns to recognize.

The next point is to see if the chair is doweled and assembled as was done in the eighteenth century. If the wood shows signs of having been sawed or planed by a mechanical device one can be sure that it is modern. Here is where wormholes play their part for most beechwood furniture is subject to the ravages of worms. Some hardwoods, such as oak and mahogany may be free of them but the undersides of beechwood chairs which have not been waxed or rubbed, as have the outsides, are rarely without some trace of wormholes. This is true of all antique woods; only veneered furniture is the exception. Real wormholes run irregularly and form zigzag tunnels under the surface, while artificial wormholes go down directly and do not deviate. Exterior horizontal galleries may have been under the surface of pieces which were originally painted and revealed when the paint was stripped off.

One must look very carefully to be sure that the apron on the underside has not been covered with a cleverly applied piece of old wood showing wormholes, while the main structure is modern. The desired impression is, of course, that the whole frame is made in one piece of the same wood, but close examination will sometimes reveal that it is glued over the new wood as a veneer is. The initials J.M.E. *(Jurande des Menuisier Ébénistes)* often accompany a genuine signature, since it was a control mark stamped on by the Corporation of Cabinetmakers when the piece, already stamped by the maker, passed through the jurisdiction of that body. Sometimes one finds the signature of the maker without the control mark, but the only explanation possible for a control mark without a master's signature is that the latter has been obliterated through the years, by repairs, accident, shrinking of the wood fibre or some other cause. The J.M.E. was at the time, a guarantee that the piece was, in fact, the work of the man who presented it to the Corporation for stamping. But furniture made to order for a definite client was frequently not stamped at all since there was no doubt as to its origin. Similarly only a few pieces in sets of furniture were stamped, as stamping them all seemed useless, but in time, when sets were broken up and the pieces separated, it left some without any identification of authorship.

Consoles are very rarely signed. They were an integral part of the room, often related to and a part of the wall paneling and made for a specific place. Thus they did not as a rule pass through the *menuisiers* guild's control. Initials branded into a piece of furniture, sometimes surmounted by a crown, indicate the royal palace or château in which it belonged. Two signatures on the same piece of furniture should not cause consternation for there are several possible explanations. One is that two cabinetmakers often collaborated on a set of furniture and both signed. Another is that a dealer bought a piece from another, possibly on the death of the author, and added his own signature because it was sold from his shop. And as mentioned before, several signatures are often found on sets of furniture where all details are identical because two or more cabinetmakers collaborated on the set.

The best antique dealer is one who loves the things he has assembled and for whom his vocation is an all-consuming hobby as well as the source of his livelihood. He generally knows a great deal more about antiques than one who is merely a shrewd merchant and buys anything he thinks he can sell at a profit. A dealer who is a collector at heart will study his material with deep interest and, as in all other occupations in life, one can only excel if one loves the profession and is willing to devote time and energy in its pursuit.

It is a curious fact that dealers like to buy furniture in

bad condition which they are obliged to repair at considerable expense. Instead of being pleased when repairs have already been undertaken and paid for by someone else, they prefer to go through the whole process themselves. Perhaps it is because in this way they know exactly what has been done or perhaps because they believe that they can have the work done better than someone else would. Whatever the reason, it is a fact that each dealer likes to prepare his own merchandise for the market.

If a painting or drawing is meticulously framed by one owner, the next pulls off the frame and changes the whole aspect of the picture. There is enormous satisfaction in putting one's personal touch into its presentation and rarely, if ever, is one satisfied by what was done by the last owner. True, styles in framing have changed and what was considered perfect years ago, looks dowdy and tasteless today. However, a great crime that has been committed within the last decade, is the way in which fine, old, hand-carved period frames have been stripped of their original gilding or covered with white gesso (plaster) and rottenstone and then rubbed, in order to allow some of the gilding to peep through. This vandalism has been perpetrated in the name of modern art for such mutilated frames are considered the ideal presentation of Impressionist paintings!

People are always searching for finds and hoping they will discover some wonderful object in an out of the way place. It is not absolutely impossible, but highly improbable that an amateur can pick up some very rare thing for the proverbial song. One finds nice little bits in the provinces in France, here and there, but they are generally priced as high, if not higher, than they would be in Paris or New York. If the amateur would only realize that whatever he is offered has already been sifted by the great dealers, by specialists in every field and even by the intermediary traveling dealers, known as *courtiers,* he would understand that if an apparently fine piece is left, it is because it was deemed false by the experts.

The famous *Marché au Pus* or flea market in Paris, as well as the Swiss Village and similar markets in London, Rome, Madrid and other large centers offer much amusement and spurious antiques *ad infinitum.* Some of the Paris dealers go to the flea market so early in the morning that almost everything really desirable is sold before some of the stands have even opened. The remaining merchandise is usually brought in from Paris shops which find it much easier, and more profitable, to do business with foreigners there in the market, than in their shops. People love going to the flea market on a lark and make purchases they would not dream of making in town or at home.

In the course of a lifetime prices fluctuate as fashions change, or as times are prosperous or the reverse. In this age of increasing production costs of contemporary furniture and reproductions; even very simple provincial antiques have risen in value over the last decade. Honest, genuine furniture of the simpler type has grown extremely difficult to find in France today and is correspondingly expensive. There is something very homelike and cozy about simple French furnishings, which are most appealing and appropriate for use in American houses, for they are gay, charming and unpretentious.

One of the surest methods of learning about antiques is to buy them with one's own money for the eye is sharpened by the expenditure of personal funds. Studying the history of art and knowing styles is most important, but some students who know a great deal in theory are very uncertain in judging a specific piece. Never having taken the risk of overextending themselves in spending their own money, they never achieve the same knowledge as one who has plunged into collecting in a practical way. On the other hand, some relatively uneducated men who deal in antiques acquire an eye and considerable ability to distinguish a good piece from a bad one. Insurance appraisers for instance, are often good at their task because of much practice, but certainly not all of them know what they are looking at. The official United States government appraisers at the Port of New York also deserve a word of praise at this point for they are extraordinarily capable in their various specialties. In France some conspicuously knowledgeable men are appointed "experts of the tribunal" or "experts of the Custom House." These are honorific titles and those on whom they have been conferred have a right to use them as titles and on their stationery, bu they are paid for their services only as and when they are called upon for their opinions.

The other so-called experts are self-appointed, as they are in the rest of the world. However, they may be as capable as those who have taken the trouble to seek official recognition for it does not follow that appointed experts never make mistakes. Infallibility does not exist, but some individuals who through great experience have attained considerable ability and judgment, come as close to the distinction as is possible.

To become a real connoisseur requires work, patience and close observation for a long period of time. Intuition plays a part, but even the quality described by this misleading word is only developed after long study and after the mind and eye have accustomed themselves to, and are filled with, the lines, colors and qualities of the material in question. One requires real knowledge as a basis of one's "flair"; otherwise it is too unreliable to be of value.

The great pieces of furniture and decorations which were made for the French Court, are the finest that have ever been produced in the world and are therefore the last word in elegance and France's triumph in the decorative arts.

There is no end of pleasure to be derived from delving into the field of French art, and it is hoped that this volume will stimulate even wider interest and prove of some assistance to those who wish to pursue the subject in greater detail than has been possible within the scope of this book.

Glossary

Accotoir or *Accoudoir:* A wooden arm support which begins at the end of the arm of a chair and extends to the seat.

Amaranth: A bright violet wood which turns brown when exposed to air.

Amboyna: An East Indian wood of light color with marked burls and swirls.

Ancien régime: Former political power.

Appliques: Wall sconces used to furnish light, usually with two or three candleholders or branches.

Apron: The band of wood, with or without a drawer, under a table top.

Arabesque: Scroll ornamentation based on plants, fruits, flowers and foliage; derived from the Arabic decorative style.

Armoire: A clothes cupboard.

Aventurine: A yellowish glass with an infinite number of brilliant little copper crystals; first made in Venice in 1720.

Banquette: A long stool.

Bergère: An armchair with upholstery enclosing the sides from arms to seat and supplied with a soft loose cushion resting on an upholstered platform.

Bibelots: Small objects of exceptional charm and interest.

Biscuit: White unglazed porcelain used extensively for groups and figures at Sèvres during the second half of the eighteenth century.

Blanc de plomb: Lead white (paint).

Bobêche: The drip cup which fits into a candleholder.

Bois de fil: See *fil de bois*.

Bois de rose: A yellowish wood striped with red which turns a mellow blonde with age.

Bois de violette: Originally called *bois violet;* see Kingwood.

Boiserie: Wood paneling.

Bombé: A curved bulbous line in furniture giving a blown out effect; a convex shape.

Bonheur-du-jour: A small writing table which first appeared after the middle of the eighteenth century, the rear portion of which is surmounted by a small cupboard for writing equipment, toilet articles or bibelots.

Bouchon: A term used in the eighteenth century to describe the removable top over the marble of a *bouillotte* table, covered in baize on one side and leather on the other.

Bouillotte: A game.

Brocatelle: A type of lampas characterized by marked relief of the design, resulting from the use of a coarse linen ground weft, silk warp and pattern weft.

Broché: A silk material with a raised floral design on a silk or satin ground of contrasting color.

Bronze d'meublement: Bronze mounts for furniture.

Bronzier: A worker in bronze.

Brûle parfum: An incense burner.

Buhl: Nineteenth-century word describing tortoise shell and brass inlay furniture in the style of André-Charles Boulle.

Bureau plat: A flat writing table or desk, usually having several drawers.

Bureau en dos d'ane: A drop-leaf desk which derives its name from an ass's back which it resembles in shape.

Cabriole leg: A leg which curves out from the seat of a piece of furniture and in again before reaching the foot where it is again parallel to the seat.

Cabriolet: A Louis XV chair with a concave back and cabriole legs.

Cache pot: A decorative flowerpot holder.

Camaïeu: Monochrome; one color in several shades.

Canapé: A sofa.

Canapé à corbeille: A sofa with in-curving ends suggesting a basket.

Capital: The head or top of a column, pilaster or pillar.

Caquetoire or caqueteuse: A type of wooden armchair of which the front is wider than the back; a shape known in France only during the sixteenth century.

Carnet: A notebook.

Cartel: A hanging wall clock.

Cartonnier: A piece of furniture created to hold papers, frequently made to stand at or on the end of a flat desk.

Cartoon: A precise drawing to be copied in tapestry or other medium.

Cassolette: A covered vase in the shape of an urn, often with reversible top which forms a candle socket.

Causeuse: A small sofa, or a large chair, similar to a marquise. Term derived from the French verb *causer*, meaning to chat.

Celadon: A light green color which is associated with Chinese porcelain.

Chaire: Choir stall.

Chauffeuse: A low chair, used by the fire. Originally a chair low enough for the knees to be slightly higher than the legs, so as to cradle a baby while changing it.

Chef-d'oeuvre: A masterpiece.

Chenets: The French name for andirons, or in England, firedogs.

Chenille: A tufted silk thread used in weaving. It is cut and twisted to produce the effect of velvet in relief, and derives its name from the word for caterpillar, which it resembles.

Chiffonier: A high chest of drawers, ranging from a small piece for odds and ends to a full-sized bedroom piece to hold clothing.

Chinoiserie: Objects produced in Europe, in the Chinese style or of Chinese inspiration. A term never applied to anything produced in China itself.

Chutes: The bronze pieces which protected and decorated the angles and legs on commodes, tables, desks and other fine furniture from the Louis XIV period on.

Cire-perdue: "Lost wax," a term applied to the wax mold which was destroyed in casting bronze.

Ciseleur: Chiseler and chaser of metal.

Citronnier: Lemonwood, which is a pale honey color when used as veneer and polished.

Cockade: A ribbon shaped into a badge; very much in use during the French Revolution.

Coiffeuse: Dressing table, deriving its name from its use in dressing hair; a synonym for *poudreuse.*

Commode: A chest of drawers.

Commode en tombeaux: A chest of drawers with short legs, the body of which almost rests on the floor; typical of the early Louis XV style.

Console: A table used against a wall as a bracket; or sometimes with legs and a stretcher.

Console leg: Bracket-shaped scroll legs.

Coromandel lacquer: A Chinese lacquer consisting of many coats of paint each of which is dried, hardened and polished before application of another. The background is dark and thick with a tendency to turn brown; decorated in bright colors, showing people, houses, mountains, etc. on a rather large, bold scale and subsequently engraved. Most French commodes in this material were made from Chinese screens.

Cuivre doré: Copper gilt.

Damask: A woven silk material usually of a single color with a satin ground on which the pattern is without sheen. The back shows the same pattern in reverse, in satin on a matte ground. The design is formed by a contrast of weave.

Dauphine: A rich silk fabric with a matte finish.

Décapage: The process of removing paint or gilding.

Desserte: A sideboard with an undershelf which first appeared in the Louis XVI period.

Doreur: Gilder of metal or wood.

Dossier plat: Flat-back; a term used to describe the back of a chair.

Dragée: A sweet; often the sugar coated almonds given guests at weddings.

Ébéniste: A cabinetmaker of quality whose craft is distinguished from that of a carpenter by his knowledge and handling of fine woods.

Ebony: A hard, fine-grained black wood. Found in hot tropical climates and used largely in France during the Louis XIV period and again under Louis Philippe.

Écran: A firescreen, also a small screen on a table or a candlestick.

Églomisé: Painting on glass, done on the reverse, frequently with gold leaf.

En cas: A small table with a drawer or cabinet.

Encoignure: Corner-cupboard.

Escutcheon: A metal keyhole ornament.

Espagnolette: A decorative motif showing a female head wearing a large stiff lacy collar or ruff such as those worn in Spain. A form of decoration used largely for bronze mounts and wood carved details in the Régence period.

Etagère: A piece of furniture composed of a number of shelves which hang on the wall. Sometimes supplied with a small cupboard at the bottom. This term which is of nineteenth-century origin is also applied to *table à ouvrage* (work table) with several shelves.

Faïence: French term for pottery.

Faïence blanche: White faïence.

Fasces: A form of decoration representing a bundle of sticks bound together, derived from the emblem of ancient Rome.

Fauteuil de bureau: Desk chair, usually of a rounded form with one leg directly in the center, two at each side and one in the middle of the back, with cane or leather back and leather seat cushion.

Fauteuil à chassis: An armchair with a framework which is upholstered and slips into place.

Fête Galante: An eighteenth century conception of a glamorous picnic in a romantic setting where elegantly apparelled ladies and gentlemen play musical instruments and games and engage in flirtation.

Fil de bois: Veneer used uninterruptedly in the full length of a piece of furniture.

Fil d'or or *fils d'argent:* Gilded silver and silver thread prepared in Genoa, and called *Fil de Chypre,* which was used in tapestry weaving from the Middle Ages to the eighteenth century.

Flambeau de paravent: A candlestick protected by convex glass to prevent the flame from being blown out when carried. It was fitted with a hook-like handle which fit over the top of a screen.

Fluting: A form of decoration in which channels or grooves run parallel to each other on a column or chair leg. A very popular motif in the Louis XVI period derived from the ancient classic forms, which were originally in marble.

Fondeur: Caster of metal.

Gadrooned: A design for the edges of metal pieces, similar to beading but with the elements elliptical instead of round and running up and down along the base or edge; widely used in the Louis XIV period and again in the nineteenth century.

Garland: Wreath of flowers or leaves; a motif which was very much in vogue during the Louis XVI period.

Gimp: A woven silk braid in different twisted designs used in finishing upholstered furniture and also as trimming on hangings and bedspreads.

Girandole: A candleholder with many branches which create a brilliant effect resembling fireworks, when lighted.

Gouache: A type of paint similar to watercolor in which albumen replaces water and gives a softer, thicker effect. Much in use in the eighteenth century; often on parchment. The Italian term for it is "tempera."

Gris Trianon: White paint used for The Trianon, now turned gray from dirt and patina of time.

Guéridon: A small round table made to support a candlestick or candelabrum. The name derives from a Moorish galley slave named Guéridon. The term is now used for any circular table.

Guéridon à crémaillière: A tiny, round table or candlestand with a marble top, a gilt bronze gallery and an adjustable ratchet support on three spreading feet; generally made in mahogany in the Louis XVI period.

Habillée: A term used to describe a picture in which fabric is pasted on as clothing and upholstery.

Hêtre: Beechwood, the chief wood employed for fine French eighteenth-century chairs.

Housse: Slip cover.

Jardinière: A decorative container for flowers.

Kakiemon: A design of Japanese character named after a family which created it; later copied all over Europe and erroneously called Korean decoration.

Kaolin: A special type of clay indispensable in the production of hard paste porcelain.

Kingwood: A coarse-grained wood, varying in hardness, of a very dark purplish brown or black color sometimes striped with black or brown.

Lacquer: The process of applying many layers of paint and a special varnish which takes a very hard polish.

Lambrequin: A valance frequently scalloped and fringed, which was used over curtains. The form was also used in designs of fabrics and in many other materials, and was often copied in carved wood or metal, as a decoration.

Lampas: A name applied to all figured textiles; in the Louis XVI period a silk fabric with a design woven in two or more tones of the same color on a contrasting satin ground.

Le Lever: The ceremony of the King's rising in the morning, which was attended by the Court.

Liseuse: A reading table with a collapsible bookrest in the center of the top.

Lisière: Selvedge, the outside border of a textile or tapestry.

Lit de repos à crosse: A day-bed with outward curled scroll ends.

Livre: The unit of money used in France before the introduction of the decimal system in coinage.

Livres d'Heures: "Book of Hours." Illuminated prayer books with prayers for certain hours. Use by laymen was prohibited until the late-fourteenth or early-fifteenth century.

Marchand bijoutière: An eighteenth-century name for a jeweller who also dealt in other precious things such as mounted objects and bibelots of all kinds.

Marquetry: Veneered woodwork sometimes inlaid in very elaborate designs and varicolored woods.

Marquise: A small sofa or large armchair.

Menuisier: A worker in solid wood rather than veneer. He also made carved consoles and all forms of decoration other than veneers.

Méridienne: A type of short sofa on which one can recline in a half-sitting position; but cannot lie down full length; usually with one end much higher than the other.

Merisier: Cherrywood. The French term for light, smooth fruitwood.

Meubles à Hauteur D'Appui: A low cupboard, bookcase or secrétaire upon which one can lean.

Meubles à transformations: Furniture which serves two or more purposes, often with mechanical devices.

Mille fleurs: Term used to designate tapestries made at the end of the fifteenth and early sixteenth century, the background of which is covered with flowers.

Moquette: A woven wool fabric with a high pile. A term used today in France for any wool carpet.

Nécessaire: Small case containing writing equipment or toilet accessories.

Ormolu: Gilded metal.

Os de mouton: Mutton bone, a term used for the legs and arms of furniture in the Louis XIII period.

Palissandre: See Kingwood.

Papier peint: Printed wallpaper which simulates painting.

Paravent: A screen.

Passamenterie: An elaborate form of braid used in upholstery and also as a trimming on clothing.

Pâte tendre: Soft paste porcelain.

Pliant: A folding stool with crossed legs.

Poêle: A stove.

Poinçon: Hallmark.

Polychrome: Many-colored.

Pomponne or *cuivre doré:* Gilded copper. The name derives from the Hôtel de Pomponne where plated and gilded ware was made.

Point de Chaînette: An eighteenth-century form of chain stitch embroidery now commercially called *Point de Beauvais.*

Pot au fard: A cosmetic pot.

Poudre d'écaille: A highly-colored substance formed of powdered tortoise shell.

Poudreuse: Powder table; a lady's dressing table, synonym for *coiffeuse.*

Rafraîchissoir: A table with shelves, a small drawer and two metal containers for cold water in which to cool wine bottles.

Réchampi: Decoration in relief, either gilded or painted in different tones or in a combination of gilt and paint.

Régence: The period between 1715 and 1723, after the death of Louis XIV and before Louis XV was of age, during which France was governed by the Duke of Orléans. Not to be confused with the English Regency which is of much later date.

Régulateur: A long case clock, or grandfather clock.

Rocaille: A decoration based on the use of shell forms and rock formations.

Servante: A serving table, sometimes round and often with several tiers; usually of the Louis XVI period.

Siège episcopal: A metal church stool.

Stile: An outside vertical member of a commode or cabinet which frames the drawers or panels.

Stretcher: A wooden support on a table, chair or other furniture, which is attached to the legs for strength and/or decoration.

Tableaux tentures: A set of wallpaper panels in the form of a picture or series of scenes of the same subject.

Table à ouvrage: A worktable. The eighteenth-century term applied to any small table with drawers or undershelf, often with spaces for writing equipment in top drawer.

Table de Chevet: Bedside table.

Tabouret: A stool.

Tapestry: A pictorial wall hanging in wool with the pattern woven in by means of colored woof threads; not to be confused with any other form of wool or silk fabric.

Tempera: See gouache.

Tenture: Term usually applied to a series or set of tapestries of one subject.

Tirette: A pull-out slide under a table or desk top which provides additional surface.

Toile: Linen or canvas.

Toile de Jouy: White or tan linen or fine cotton with scenes printed in red, violet or brown.

Torchère: A tall, round candle or candelabrum holder.

Tricoteuse: A small worktable with a gallery, one side of which is often hinged and can be lowered, and frequently with two shelves besides the top. A form first developed in the Louis XVI period and continued through the Directoire and thereafter.

Trictrac: Backgammon.

Trompe l'Oeil: A device in painting, wood-working or other media, which deceives the eye.

Trophies: Decorations composed of war accoutrement.

Tulipwood: A rather hard, densely grained wood of light color with a definite red grain suggesting red and white tulips.

Velour d'Utrecht: A wool velvet first produced in Utrecht, Holland and very widely used in the seventeenth century.

Veneer: A thin slice of any fine wood which is applied to plain unfinished wood furniture and then highly polished to produce an elegant and brilliant effect.

Verdure: A tapestry which is predominantly green, showing

woods, meadows, bushes and trees with an occasional figure, animal or bird.

Vermeil: Silver gilt.

Vernis Martin: A very fine lacquer perfected, but not invented by the Martin brothers, who were granted a patent in 1730, allowing them the exclusive right to imitate lacquer in relief in the Chinese and Japanese manner.

Verre de fougère: Fern glass; very light glass with a greenish tinge.

Voyeuse: A chair which a man straddles leaning his arms on the upholstered back. Similar to an English cock-fighting chair, made to be used in watching card games.

Warp: The set of threads which run lengthwise in the weaving of fabrics; sometimes of a different material than the woof.

Woof: The yarn running crosswise in a fabric or at right angles to the warp threads. Presently known as weft in England and filling in America.

CHRONOLOGY

	REIGNED BETWEEN
Charles VI	1380–1422
Charles VII	1422–1461
Louis XI	1461–1483
Charles VIII	1483–1498
Louis XII	1498–1515
François I	1515–1547
Henri II	1547–1559
François II	1559–1560
Charles IX	1560–1574
Henri III	1574–1589
Henri IV	1589–1610
Louis XIII	1610–1643
Louis XIV	1643–1715
Régence (Duc d'Orléans)	1715–1723
Louis XV King	1715–1774
Louis XVI	1774–1792
Louis XVII Titular King	1793–1795
Directoire	1795–1799
Consulate	1799–1804
Empire (Napoleon Bonaparte)	1804–1814
Louis XVIII	1814–1824
Charles X	1824–1830
Louis Philippe	1830–1848

Bibliography

LES MEUBLES I. DE L'ART ANTIQUE AU STYLE
LOUIS XIV
Flammarion, Paris, 1929   Guillaume Janneau

LES MEUBLES II. DU STYLE RÉGENCE AU STYLE
LOUIS XVI
Flammarion, Paris 1929   Guillaume Janneau

LES MEUBLES III. DU STYLE LOUIS XVI AU
STYLE EMPIRE
Flammarion, Paris   Guillaume Janneau

LES STYLES
LOUIS XIV ET RÉGENCE DÉCORATION ET
MOBILIER
Librairie Grund/Paris, 1929
6 Rue Mazarine, Paris VIᵉ   Seymour de Ricci

FRENCH PORCELAIN OF THE EIGHTEENTH
CENTURY
Faber & Faber
24 Russell Square, London   W. B. Honey

J. B. PIGALLE
Éditions Pierre Tisne, 1950   Louis Reau

DER GOLDECHMIEDE MERKZEICHEN
Verlag Von Henrich Keller
Frankfort Am Main, 1890   Dr. Marc Rosenberg, A.O.

HISTOIRE DE LA CERAMIQUE
Paris, 1875   Albert Jacquemart

L'AMATORE DI MAIOLICHE A PORCELLANE
Ulrico Hoepli, Milano, 1924   L. De Mauri

VERSAILLES
Henri Lefebure
25 Rue du Faubourg St. Honore, 1960 Jean de La Varende

LE STYLE LOUIS PHILIPPE NAPOLEON III
Librairie Larousse, Paris VIᵉ, 1939   H. Clousot

LE SIEGE EN FRANCE
DU MOYEN AGE À NOS JOURS
Paul Hartmann, Paris, 1948   Pierre Devinoy &
Madeleine Jarry

FRENCH FAÏENCE
Faber & Faber, 1646, London   Arthur Lane

LA VERRERIE EN FRANCE DE L'ÉPOQUE
GALLO-ROMAINE A NOS JOURS
Librairie Larousse, Paris VIᵉ   James Barrelet

CONNAISSANCE DES ARTS
LE XVII SIÈCLE FRANCAISE
LE XVIII SIÈCLE FRANCAISE
LE XIX SIÈCLE FRANCAISE
Librairie Hachette 1957

LES ÉBÉNISTES DU XVIIIᵐᵉ SIÈCLE
Paris, Les Éditions D'Art Et D'Histoire 1934
Comte de Salverte

L'ART ET LE MANIÈRE DES MAÎTRES ÉBÉNISTES
FRANCAIS AU XVIIIᵉ SIÈCLE
Guy Le Prat—Éditeur
5, Rue Des Grands Augustins, Paris   Jean Nicolay

LE MEUBLE LÉGER EN FRANCE
Paul Hartman, Éditeur, Paris 1952   Guillaume Janneau

L'OEIL DU CONNAISSEUR
LES MEUBLES DU XVIIIᵉ SIÈCLE
I: MENUSIERIE
Presses Universitaires de France
108, Boulevard Saint-Germain, Paris   Pierre Verlet

L'OEIL DU CONNAISSEUR
LES MEUBLES DU XVIIIᵉ SIÈCLE
II: ÉBÉNISTERIE
Presses Universitaires de France, Paris 1956
108, Boulevard Saint-Germain, Paris   Pierre Verlet

LE STYLE RENAISSANCE
Librairie Larousse, Paris VIᵉ   François Gébelin

LE STYLE HENRY IV–LOUIS XIII
Librairie Larousse, Paris VIᵉ   Pierre du Colombier

LE STYLE LOUIS XIV
Librairie Larousse, Paris VIᵉ   Roger-Armand Weigert

LE STYLE LOUIS XV
Librairie Larousse, Paris VIᵉ   Pierre Verlet

LA GRAVURE FRANCAISE
Librairie Larousse, Paris VIᵉ   Émile Dacier

LE DESSIN FRANCAIS
Librairie Larousse, Paris VIᵉ   Pierre Lavallée

LA TAPISSERIE FRANCAISE
Librairie Larousse, 1956   Roger-Armand Weigert

L'ORFEVRERIE FRANCAISE
LA MÉDAILLE DE FRANCE
Librairie Larousse, Paris VIᵉ   Jean Babelon

LE STYLE EMPIRE
Librairie Larousse, Paris VIᵉ   Pierre Francastel
LE STYLE LOUIS-PHILLIPPE NAPOLEON III
Librairie Larousse, Paris VIᵉ   Henri Clouzot

WALLACE COLLECTION; CATALOGUE OF
FURNITURE, 1956
Hertford House, 1956, London
                F. J. B. Watson, B.A./F.S.A.

FAÏENCE FRANCAISE
Éditions Charles Massin, Paris   Y. Brunhammer

FAÏENCE DE FRANCE
Éditions de Deux-Mondes, Paris 1954   Émile Tilmans

INDEX